HOLISTIC INSIGHTS

Alternative and complemen. , confirm are here to stay within today's twenty first society.

Even though life can be so busy, fast and frenetic mother nature has her way of healing. Thankfully we really can take the time to embrace fresh vital therapies from the tremendous reservoir of alternative therapist we have available today in the whole world, let alone the United Kingdom who can compete in terms of the orthodox medical box and look beyond our current lifestyle towards natural living health.

Holistic Insights claims to be the Capitals voice for the message of today. I salute that claim and encourage finding a way to spread the message. Particularly to ordinary individuals who may suffer from ill-health which has manifested itself within their body, and assist them to know and discover for themselves the alternative choices available to them.

From the twenty-first century viewpoint, there are numerable diseases, some that are curable and then there are those that are incurable via the traditional medical route. Or are they?

Speaking from my experience touched by dis-ease, disability and loss, I will share with you the concept that there can be no incurable diseases. Therefore mind over matter does prevail. In fact the root definition of the words curable and incurable is 'cared for', meaning that if the individual takes care of one's self then good health can be established and maintained and dis-ease will not set in. That is why it is important to utilize the help of those 'other' professionals who can help us with alternative health care options.

Within the parameters of complimentary medicine both the negative and the positive influences of an individual can be treated. Particularly those individuals expressing them as ill-health symptoms, dis-ease.

The attainment of excellent health is possible and sustainable, one only needs to know how to take incredible self care, experience the gift of free will and practice mind over matter, in other words holistic insight. A qualified practitioner will be able to help this worthy goal.

Basically to live in a state of premium health it is important to enjoy a level of quality lifestyle living. To do that the whole body and mind is looked at by a qualified alternative therapy practitioner. The trick then is to coordinate both the physical and the mental abilities of the patients' with natures own healing aids.

I sincerely hope you enjoy owning this valuable publication.

Dr PaTrisha Anne
Author & Speaker on CAM issues.

HOLISTIC INSIGHTS
London Edition

ISBN: 1-903361-25-7

Published by: Kingsley Media Ltd - Plymouth
Copyright: Kingsley Media Ltd

Kingsley Media Ltd wishes to thank the advertisers and the healthcare practitioners who have contributed their support and knowledge.

The Editor wishes to thank Nikky Lea, Sandra Murton, Lynda Walker and Lorna Blood for their dedication and conscientiousness, without them this book would not have been possible, and the creative team at daddylonglegs for their professionalism and expertise.

Typeset & Graphics – daddylonglegs (www.bigonideas.com)   Concept – Melissa Willcocks PhD.
Printed by Century Print   Editor - Louise O'Neill.

CONTENTS

Medical Acupuncture is a safe and effective method of treatment for many common ailments, it encourages the body to promote natural healing and improve functioning, by inserting very thin needles and applying heat or electrical stimulation at procise acupuncture points.

How Does Acupuncture Work?

The Chinese explanation is that channels of energy run in regular patterns through the body and over its surface. These energy channels, called meridians, are like rivers flowing through the body to irrigate and nourish the tissues. An obstruction in the movement of these energy rivers is like a dam that backs up the flow in one part of the body and restricts it in others.

The meridians can be influenced by needling the acupuncture points. The Acupuncture needles unblock the obstruction at the dams, and re-establish the regular flow through the meridians. Acupuncture treatments can therefore help the body's internal organs to correct imbalances in their digestion, absorption, and energy production activities. Acupuncture can also help in the circulation of energy through the meridians.

The modern scientific explanation is that needling the acupuncture points stimulates the nervous system to release chemicals in the muscles, spinal cord, and brain. These chemicals will either change the experience of pain, or they will trigger the release of other chemicals and hormones which influence the body's own internal regulating system. The improved energy and biochemical balance produced by acupuncture results in stimulation of the body's own natural healing abilities, and in promoting physical and emotional well-being.

Have you tried everything else?

With acupuncture, the patient will not have to learn to live with an ailment. Many patients have been told to see a psychiatrist because no physiological disorder can be found or treated by known methods, even though the patient fervently attests that he/she is in tremendous pain or discomfort. Sometimes they are simply told to learn to live with it. Something can be done and has been done, because acupuncture has helped in cases where other methods of treatment have failed. Acupuncture treats the causes as well as the symptoms of an illness.

How many treatments will I need?

The number of treatments needed differs from person to person. For more complex or long standing conditions, two or three treatments a week for several months may be recommended. For acute problems, usually fewer visits are required. For health maintenance, one treatment a month may be all that is necessary.

Afraid of needles? – No need to worry.

People experience acupuncture needles differently. Some patients feel no pain at all when the needles are inserted, and some patients experience minimal pain. Once the needles are in place, there is no pain felt. Acupuncture needles are very thin and solid, and are made from stainless steel. The point of the needle is smooth (Acupuncture needles are smooth, not hollow like hypodermic needles. Hollow needles increases the risk of skin bruising and skin irritation.), and insertion through the skin is not as painful as injections or blood sampling.

Alexander Technique

The Alexander Technique is a successful way to solve body problems. It's a way of learning how you can get rid of harmful tension by changing how you habitually carry out your everyday activities. This practical method will improve your ease and freedom of movement, reduce tension and improve your balance, support and coordination.

How can the Alexander Technique help you?

Many people develop back neck and shoulder pain and tight limbs and feel generally that their posture is bad. They may also believe that problems in their joints and muscles are unchangeable. However, as they learn the Technique, they find that it really can make lasting positive changes resulting in improved movement.

We all have unconscious movement habits and without realising we put undue pressure on ourselves. We collapse as we sit and over tighten our shoulders and use more force than is necessary to grip objects. We blame problems on activities but often it is how we do something that creates the problem, not the activity itself. This excess tension often starts in childhood and if left unchecked, can lead later in life to common ailments such as arthritis, neck and back pain, migraines, sciatica, and breathing difficulties.

An Alexander Technique teacher can help you to see how you might be causing your recurring difficulties, whether it's back pain, neck or shoulder tension, restricted breathing, headaches, or simply feeling uncomfortable in your body. Analysing your whole movement pattern, not just your symptoms, the teacher helps you to become aware of your habits of compression and tightness in you everyday activities such as sitting, standing and walking. You can then learn to strip away harmful habits, have more self awareness and make new conscious choices in order to restore your original posture and poise. You come to understand how your body works and how to make it work better for you.

What happens in a lesson?

The Alexander Technique is taught on a one-to-one basis. During a lesson your teacher will observe your posture and movement patterns and will use her hands to help unravel distortions and tensions while guiding your body into a place of balance and poise. The touch used is very gentle, is totally non invasive and you

do not need to remove any clothing. Since some work is generally done while you are lying down on a table it's advisable for women to wear comfortable trousers.

You will be asked to follow what is happening and be involved in the process although sometimes it's so relaxing that there is a temptation to fall asleep!

How long are lessons and how many will you need?

A lesson usually lasts between thirty minutes and one hour. The majority of people take between twenty and forty lessons and then come back for refresher lesson from time to time. Regular lessons are recommended initially in order to gain the maximum benefit.

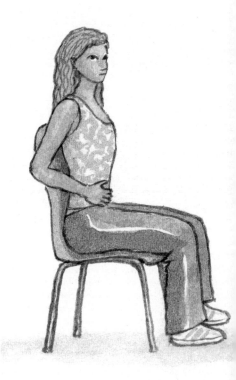

Paul Harland RGN, MSTAT, Brixton SW2. Tel: 0207 737 6328.Web: www.alextec.info . E-mail: paulharland@alextec.info. Over twenty years teaching, including actors and musicians at national theatre, Westminster School. Continuous private practice for individual lessons.

The Alexander Technique in Balham and Clapham. William Shepherd MSTAT. 19 Terrapin Road, London, SW17 8QN And St.Luke's Community Hall (off Nightingale Lane) 020 8673 6598 & 07703219182.

Carol Summers, MSTAT, Teaching The Alexander Technique from Newport Road, Leyton, E10 & Bloomsbury Alexander Centre, Southampton Row, WC1. Tel: 020 8539 5769/ 07929 410055, Email: c.summers@bushinternet.com

Aromatherapy

Aromatherapy is simply a holistic therapy using aromatic oils, its use and effect is very similar to Homeopathy where the whole body is treated as a physiological and psychological experience. To achieve total success the art is with the therapist to use the most effective oils to create an ambience of trust and professionalism with the client, thus bringing out the healing energy which will help the client to regain a sense of feeling well, with the return of abundant energy.

How Can Aromatherapy Help You?

Being an established treatment aromatherapy has proven benefits for many ailments, for instance:
Emotionally based benefits: Depression, Frustration, Grief, Hysteria, Anxiety, Insomnia, Mood Swings and the many ancillary effects any of these conditions can bring.

Medicinal benefits: Bruises, Burns (including sunburn), Nervousness, Tension and Stress, Car - Air or Sea Sickness, Respiratory Conditions including colds, flu, sore throat, asthma and bronchitis. Muscular aches and pains, fungal infections such as athletes foot and nail fungus and skin inflammation.
Skincare benefits: Dermatitis, Stretch Marks, Eczema, Acne, Psoriasis, Mature Skin, Varicose Veins, Dry Skin, Cellulite and anti-ageing.

By learning more about the proper use of essential oils through a qualified aromatherapy practitioner, you will open the door to a whole new world, one that is not so dependent on antibiotics and other over-prescribed drugs.

Aromatherapy is not intended to replace traditional medicine or traditional healthcare. It is simply an avenue for you to take more responsibility for your own health and to allow nature to do what it doe best– balance and heal body, mind and spirit.

Before purchasing essential oils for home use, it i always best to seek the advice of a professiona /qualified aromatherapy practitioner.
Avoid The Following Oils When Pregnant: Basil Cedarwood, Clary Sage, Fennel, Jasmine, Juniper Lavender, Marjoram, Myrrh, Rose, Rosemary Sage, and Thyme.
Avoid the following oils if you have Epilepsy Camphor, Fennel, Hyssop, Sage, and Rosemary.

Ways of using aromatherapy:

● Place a few drops of essential oil into a bow of steaming water. Breathe the steam for 15-30 minutes. This is great for clearing sinuses an providing cold relief.

● Mix your favourite essential oil(s) with distille water (no more than 15 drops of oil(s) per ounc of water) for a refreshing floral spray...

● Place a few drops on a cloth. Use this cloth a a scarf or place it on your pillowcase. Move clot away when you have had enough.

● Use during massage. This can have amazin effects. Beware that changes can happe EXTREMELY fast when doing this, so dilution i recommended.

● Aromatherapy bath salts are often bot extremely relaxing and effective.

Aura-Soma is a holistic soul therapy in which the vibrational of powers of colour, crystals and natural aromas combine with light in order to harmonise body, mind and spirit of mankind.

"Aura" refers to the electromagnetic field which surrounds our body and which can be seen by sensitive people. "Soma" means body.

Aura-Soma was "discovered" by the Englishwoman Vicky Wall in the mid-eighties. Vicky was a clairvoyant who realised early on in her life that she possessed a special gift: she could see people's auras. One night in her laboratory she collected together a wealth of natural ingredients, thereby discovering the contents of the Equilibrium bottles. Later she said that her hands had been led. All the ingredients were from the mineral and plant kingdom, as well as from the realm of light and colour. In the course of her life she discovered that people tended to choose bottles of the same colours as their own aura. That was a surprise for her.

The benefit of Aura Soma is recognising one's own path in life, following it and also being able to support and accompany others on their path. Striving for a communication of the emotions in order to be able to express what we really feel, think and wish for, without causing harm to others. Learning to take more and more responsibility for ourselves and thereby recognising that in precisely this attitude lies the chance for the planet and the future of mankind. Striving for unconditional love, thus opening up our consciousness to the far-reaching changes taking place on our planet. Each one of us is invited to contribute, according to our skills and natural abilities, to helping make the earth once again a place where all forms of existence can co-exist in peace, harmony and love.

The Equilibrium bottles are the central aspect of Aura-Soma. They usually consist of two different colours. The top part of the bottle consists of a colour in an oil base, the bottom part of a colour in a water base. The oily part floats on top of the watery part and there is a clear division between the two. When the bottle is shaken vigorously an emulsion exists for a moment which has the colour of the two parts mixed together. It is wonderful to watch how the colours merge and then separate out again. The two coloured liquids also look beautiful without being shaken. One feels instinctively drawn to the clear, intensive, shining colours. After shaking the bottle you apply a few drops to the skin. The exact location on the body differs from bottle to bottle and depends on the colour combination of the particular bottle. This application enables the energies in the bottle to be absorbed by the body.

An Aura-Soma treatment occurs as follows:
From the 101 Equilibrium oils one chooses 4 bottles to which, for some reason, one feels particularly drawn. The first bottle chosen shows our life task. This is the purpose with which we have incarnated. The second bottle points to the greatest difficulties, and, when we have worked on them and overcome them, the greatest gift we can receive. The third bottle shows how far along our path we have already travelled. The fourth bottle points to future perspectives.

An Aura-Soma practitioner will then be able to tell you something about each of the bottles chosen. A reading lasts about an hour.

"I picked the bottles which contained the colours I like – turquoise, emerald green, purple, orange and red. It was quite amazing to learn that these colours corresponded to exactly where I was in my life, where I wanted to go and what I needed to work on to get there. Amazing – all that from colours in bottles!" **By Aura Soma Practitioner Sue Routner**

What Is Autogenic Therapy?

Autogenic Therapy (AT) is a powerful and comprehensive therapeutic system encompassing both mind and body. Autogenic Therapy teaches skills enabling clients to utilise their own capacity for self-healing and self-development.

The core of AT is a training course during which clients learn a series of simple exercises in body awareness and relaxation designed to switch off the stress-related "fight and flight" system of the body and switch on the "rest, relaxation and recreation" system. During training the client has the opportunity to learn and experience passive concentration, a state of alert but detached awareness which enables the trainee to break through the vicious circle of excessive stress, whatever its origins.

Once learnt, these techniques form a life-long skill which can become part of a health-promoting lifestyle. They require no special clothing or difficult postures.

women to enhance performance, to airline pilots and crew to combat jet lag and fatigue, and in the business environment to optimise performance and concentration and reduce stress.
By: The British Autogenic Society.

Gill suffered from stress, inability to cope with pressure, sleepless nights and anxiety. Also high blood pressure. After 1 sesion only, she reported marked improvement. On completion, her blood pressure was lower than ever much to the surprise of her GP. Gill: "AT and Tammy have changed my life" **by therapist Tammy Mindel**

"I did AT before having a mastectomy. It helped me get through it calmly and feel positive." ST, Mother

"AT is there for me in my darkest times and when things are going well. I think of it as a cross between meditation and self-hypnosis. It's wonderful." PM, Writer

"AT has helped me to find a balance physically and emotionally despite external pressures. I feel less at the mercy of my environment." JL, Social Worker

"Since learning AT I have greater confidence and my skin's improving too." KP, Actress

Testimonials by Katey D'Ancona

Learn Autogenic Training for profound relaxation and personal growth in comfortable environment with Dr. Alice Green, London W1. Tel: 020 75804188 or visit www.dralicegreen.com

Bates Method

Seeing is a delicate process involving the mind as well as the eyes. It can be affected by stress and illness, as well as by the effort of straining to see under the wrong conditions.

A Bates teacher will help you to become aware of strain, so that you can practise being relaxed. You learn various techniques: palming for relaxation and mental focus, shifting and swinging to increase your awareness, and various ways of improving co-ordination. You learn that seeing depending on being able to remember images and imagine them changing, without trying to force them to change. Much work is done with the eyes closed.

Unlike most therapies, Bates method is not about going to a practitioner to be worked on until you are better. It is about learning to take charge of your own visual process, to understand cause and effect within yourself, and to move towards a new way of seeing and being.

How long this will take, and how far you will get with it, cannot be predicted, but it is definitely possible to increase, visual acuity to 20/20 and beyond with Bates method. All kinds of eyesight difficulties can be helped, and the progress of degenerative disease can be slowed.

Wearing glasses or contact lenses can be compared to using crutches. They prop up the underlying condition, they never cure it. Some people seem to be perfectly happy with glasses, but others find that they get headaches and eyestrain, or their prescription gets stronger over the years until they wonder where it will end. These are the ones who will be motivated to explore Bates method, which takes some dedication and willingness to change, and may also throw up underlying emotional problems which will need to be addressed.

There is nothing like the thrill of getting a clear flash and realising that what is usually out of focus for you has suddenly become visible without any effort at all. It is a kind of clarity that cannot be achieved with glasses, because there is an absence of strain and an immediacy which makes the world seem so much more real. Progress tends to consist of clear flashes which become longer and more stable as the student gets the feel for it.

Francesca Gilbert GBC, LCHE, RSHom.
Registered Bates Method Teacher and Registered Homeopath. Kingston, Putney and Wimbledon
Learn to see more clearly
020 8549 9246 / 07813 777408
email: visualeyeshealth@aol.com

Nora Matthews BA
Bates Method of Vision Education, GSVE
Reflexology, IFR, Reiki Master. Neasden
NW London. Phone: 020 8452 3473
email: nora_matthews@yahoo.co.uk

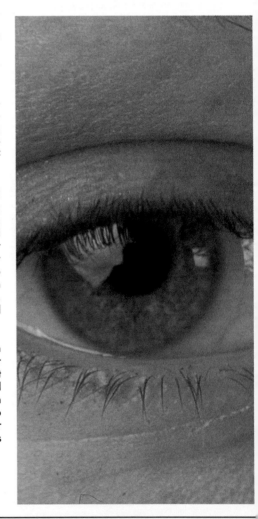

Bi-Aura Energy-Therapy

We are born bursting with life and yet grow old depleted of vitality. We are a miniature field of the electro-magnetic field of the universe and steps must be taken to recapture this vital force.

It has been known for thousands of years and recorded in early Chinese documents dating from the time of the Yellow Emperor that electric "Energy" has become the buzz word – but then what do we understand by that? Is it all "hocus pocus" or is there some scientific basis to it all? As more and more people look towards Alternative Medicine to solve their health problems, the field is so vast that it's no wonder that confusion sets in.

The current research in Quantum Physics and Parapsychology clearly demonstrates that we are just in the beginning stages of understanding our World.
Einstein's equation $E = Mc_$ tells us that matter is Energy. Everything on this planet breaks down into sub-atomic particles - ENERGY! More importantly – our own bodies are Energy. We are all Energy co-existing and interacting in a world vibrating with Energy and each of us is influencing and contributing to the overall Energy around us.

Physicists working at the Government Testing laboratories in White Sands, New Mexico isolated the smallest particle of Energy – a unit far smaller than an atom – in a sealed cloud chamber. Nothing else could get in – and the particle certainly couldn't get out. Too small to be seen by the human eye – it was photographed on ultra sensitive film. In the cloud chamber, this particle had a measurable size, weight, speed and pattern. It remained constantly in motion until eventually falling to the bottom of the chamber. It appeared to die! The camera was left rolling and soon the tiny unit of energy was back, but at a new size and weight, moving in a new pattern and speed. The conclusion from this experiment was that Energy does not die - it transforms!

Our bodies should be filled with Energy but stresses of day-to-day living create blocks within us.

currents flow through certain pathways – "meridians" in the body. These electric currents are connected to the nervous system and thus on to every organ, tissue and cell in the body. It follows that whenever there is an electric current flowing in a human being – a bio-magnetic field is created which permeates and surrounds that body.

Much scientific research has been done to measure these electrical fields. A device called SQUID (super conducting quantum interference device) was used by Dr. John Zimmerman at the University of Colorado School of Medicine to measure the bio-magnetic fields of various parts of the body – i.e. brain, heart and many other organs. These readings are very useful in understanding how the body works and in diagnosing illness. It was found that this electric field did not stop at the skin – but emanated beyond into the aura – i.e. the space surrounding the skin. It would then follow that the hands also have a bio-magnetic field surrounding and emanating from them. So – when a Healer places his/her hands near a sick organ – the bio-magnetic field emanating from

The hands are much stronger than that of the sick organ and will begin pulsating at the frequency needed by such organ. An adjustment is then induced in the frequency of the electrical current flowing in the cells and nervous system around the organ and healing takes place.

Being composed of Energy – it makes sense that Energy can heal us, so for those searching for a way to prevent ill-health and heal without dangerous drugs and their negative side-effects – the success over the last few years in the treatment of many serious illnesses would indicate the super-effectiveness of Bio-Energy.
Editorial donated by - Joanna Kyriakis

Biodanza

Feeling fed up? Anxious? Stressed out?
Finding it difficult to cope with life's demands? Why not gift yourself with Biodanza Classes?
How would you like to experience uplifting dances with inspirational music from around the world? Biodanza enabled me to connect with my true potential and express it through dance. It is, for me, an invitation to join in the Great Cosmic Dance of Life that goes on continuously in our universe – a universe that's held in the embrace of the Great Spirit. Biodanza enables us to restore the flow of harmony and peace to our universe.

Through the combination of selected inspirational music, dance and affective connection with others, profound and subtle healing takes place. The exercises in Biodanza are especially designed by Rolando Toro, (creator of The Biodanza System) to develop the potential within each of us and awaken our dormant energy and giftedness. A Biodanza session begins the process of gently opening our hearts to release the tensions in our body and as we enter into this process, life takes on new meaning. We connect with the sacred within ourselves, the other and all of life.

Dancing for wholeness is probably the oldest spiritual path to wholeness known to humanity. Organic music has the capacity of opening a door into the soul. Music can rightly be called the universal language as it evokes, creates, and echoes the deepest longings of our lives. In Biodanza, music is the royal way to enter into each exercise – it is the heart of Biodanza.
My dream is that together in Biodanza will co-create a sustainable future where everyone and everything will live in peace and harmony as we dance our way to paradise.
By Catherine Mc Inerney.

"I have suffered with angina, asthma and anxiety for years. Through Biodanza, I have learned to 'let go' of that wall of protection I had built around me for years. I can now 'go with the flow' of Life & live each day with openness to opportunity for meaningful living. I feel more energetic, confident and free. I've stopped throwing stones on my own path to wholeness. Yes, Biodanza has transformed my life. Catherine, thank you for being my teacher and angel of Biodanza"
Sue Whyte, Gastein Road, Barons Court. W6

Body Control Pilates
By Lynne Robinson

Lynne is the world's top-selling Pilates author and presenter, being co-author of three books on the Pilates Method and presenter of three Body Control Pilates videos. She features regularly in the national media and contributes to articles in the general and specialist press, Lynne is co-founder of the Body Control Pilates Teacher Training organisation and holds a BA Honours and a Postgraduate Certificate of Education.

I attended my first Pilates class whilst I was living in Sydney, Australia and, quite simply, it turned my world upside down! I had been suffering from chronic back and neck problems for five years, the result of lack of exercise, two large babies, stress and terrible posture. I had given up hope of resuming normal life. In my heart I knew that exercise held the key to restoring my health and yet aerobics and gym work were far too strenuous — even gentle yoga aggravated my problems. And then I discovered Pilates...

Within ten minutes of my first class I thought to myself, 'Where has this been all my life?' My second thought was 'Why have I never heard of Pilates before, everyone should know about it?' What I loved about it most was that not only could I do the exercises without pain but that I instantly felt differently about my body.

Joseph Pilates had promised that 'In ten sessions you'll feel the difference, in twenty you'll see the difference and in thirty you'll have a new body.' Almost instantly, I found that I was so much more aware of my posture, my breathing and, also, the deep abdominal muscles which I needed to support my spine. The regular tension headaches I had suffered with for years disappeared, as did the chronic pain in my back. I felt a new woman at 35! It wasn't long before friends started to notice the difference.

Delighted with the newfound strength in my abdominals and back, the cosmetic benefits - a flatter stomach, trimmer thighs and toned buttocks - were side effects I certainly welcomed.

Pilates had not only changed the way I looked, but also the way I felt and the way I moved. So why was it still unknown outside of the world of dancers and celebrities? For years Pilates had been "the best kept secret of the rich and famous". In the United Kingdom, for example, the few studios which existed were London-based and very exclusive. Mainly ballet dancers and performers frequented Joseph Pilates' first studio in New York, which he set up in the 1920s.

So what makes this method different to other fitness techniques? Why are the exercises so special? Well, Body Control Pilates is unlike any other exercise technique in that it actually changes the way in which you move, restoring natural, normal movement to the body. Body Control Pilates exercises are also suitable for everyone, irrespective of age and fitness level.

Essentially, Body Control Pilates is a body conditioning method which offers both mental and physical training. By improving focus and body awareness you learn how to release unnecessary tension and how to align your body correctly, with the pelvis, spine and joints all in their natural 'neutral' settings.

Next step is to learn how to breathe more efficiently, breathing into your sides and back, expanding the lower ribcage — we call this lateral thoracic breathing. You are then taught how to engage the postural muscles which stabilise the lumbar spine — in particular, the pelvic floor muscles, tranversus abdominis, and a deep back muscle called multifidus.

Once you have mastered stabilising the lumbar spine, you need to learn how to stabilise the shoulder blades, ensuring good upper body use. Relaxed, aligned, breathing correctly and with the stabilising muscles working to create a 'girdle of strength' around the trunk, you can then add movement, simple movements at first but becoming increasingly challenging as co-ordination skills develop. Light weights may then be used or resistance added with the use of specially-designed studio equipment. Each exercise is also built around the following eight key principles: Relaxation, Concentration, Alignment, Breathing, Centring, Co-ordination, Flowing Movements, Stamina.

By practising the exercises regularly (for about three hours per week) sound movement patterns are encouraged, your body will be gently realigned

Body Control Pilates

lifetime pilates

1 to1 private tuition & relaxing mat work classes 4 days a week in Blackheath, Greenwich, Lee & West Wickham

Pilates is <u>total</u> body conditioning for anyone of any age

Mother and Daughter

BODY CONTROL PILATES
Qualified Instructors

Sue 07970 053 951
Sharon 07932 735 716

BODY CONTROL PILATES is a registered Trade Mark used under licence

and reshaped and the muscles balanced, so that the whole body moves efficiently. The exercises also help to improve the circulatory, respiratory and lymphatic systems. By bringing together body and mind and by heightening body awareness, Body Control Pilates literally teaches you to be in control of your body, allowing you to handle stress more effectively and achieve relaxation more easily,

For more information on Body Control Pilates or for details of your nearest qualified teacher, please send an sae to Body Control Pilates, 14 Neal's Yard, London, WC2H 9DP or visit the website at www.bodycontrol.co.uk

---

**Sharon Eva Degen
Body Control Pilates" Qualified ITEC Dip.
Therapeutic 'One-to-One' Pilates Lessons,
Delivered to your Door
Tufnell Park, Highgate, Northern Line &
Surrounding Areas
Call 020-7272-9458**

Sally Marshall

Battersea & Wandsworth Area
For information on one to one
& group sessions call sally Marshall on:
0207 2232087
Or
07710 306 297
sally_marshall1@btinternet.com

Body Control Pilates
with the Holistic Company

If you have a bad back, poor mobility, are recovering from a sports injury, want a flatter tummy, want to strengthen your body, improve posture, relieve tension and stress then pilates will help

Fun and friendly classes. Small group sizes ensuring you get the correct level of attention.

For more information call: 020 72287344 or e-mail: jacqui@theholisticcompany.co.uk
Also available: private 1-1 and small group sessions, advice on dietary matters

Maybe you're a grandfather or a mother of 4 like me.
Pilates is a method for everyone.

**Make it work for you with a
Body control certified instructor**
Tel: 07780614265   www.pilateswithzoe.com

Simply stated, the Bowen Technique allows the body to reset and heal itself. A Bowen treatment consists of a series of gentle moves on skin (or through light clothing); with the client usually lying on a bed or comfortable treatment couch. A treatment session usually lasts from half an hour to an hour and frequently results in a deep sense of overall relaxation, allowing the body to recharge and balance itself.

Recent studies have shown the beneficial effects of deep levels of relaxation on our immune and hormonal systems. However, the Bowen Technique can also be extremely effective for musculo-skeletal problems such as back pain and sports injuries.
There are many theories as to how the Bowen Technique works, but none that completely explain its holistic effect and often outstanding results. The body is a highly complex unit dependent upon the balance of all its aspects. Whilst the orthodox medical profession still tend to take a symptomatic view of disease, Bowen is truly holistic in its approach. One Bowen move may address the entire system producing maximum results with minimal intervention.

Unlike some other hands-on disciplines, the Bowen Technique does not impose a particular approach on the client. Instead, it encourages a gentle response which empowers the body's own resources to heal itself. Bowen moves are, in themselves, a study in delicacy, being light, gentle and very precise. Frequent pauses between moves give the body time to respond and benefit.
When you go to a Bowen therapist for the first time, he or she will take a thorough case history. As with any holistic therapy, the patient may be expected to take some personal responsibility for their recovery and well-being. They may, for example, be asked to practise some simple exercises or make small adjustments to diet, avoid other forms of manipulative treatment and allow the body time for the technique to work.

The Bowen Technique is not necessarily a 'long-term' treatment programme. Most clients find that a small number of treatments are adequate even for long-standing complaints. A Bowen therapist will not recommend anything that would contravene the advice of your doctor. In fact Bowen therapists are happy to consult with doctors and explain the treatment approach if necessary. You do not need to be unwell to benefit from Bowen therapy, as it is an effective way to help the body function at an optimal level of health.

How can The Bowen Technique help? The Bowen Technique is considered safe to use on anyone, from new-born babies to the elderly and can be used where other therapies might be considered unsafe, such as during pregnancy or after a recent operation or injury. Some of the wide range of conditions that may respond well to a Bowen treatment are;

● Sports injuries, Stress & Tension symptoms, Back pain and Sciatica, RSI & Tennis Elbow,
● Neck & Shoulder problems, Knee & Ankle problems, Asthma & Hayfever, Menstrual irregularities
● Migraines & Headaches, Chronic viral fatigue syndrome & M.E., Pregnancy & Childhood disorders

Sports professionals the world over have been treated successfully with Bowen Therapy. Tests have shown that they show consistently higher performance output and an accelerated rate of recovery from injury after Bowen treatments.

Claire (not her real name), a 25 year old nurse, attended the clinic presenting with chronic lower back pain that had started after a road traffic accident 7 years previously. She was suffering from numbness in her right hip and leg, severe period pain and a severe pain in the left kidney area of her back.

She was able to attribute these symptoms to a restricted sacro-iliac joint on her left side and general compression through the lower lumbar area following visits to various consultants and x-

The Bowen Technique

ray tests. On assessment, I found that there was a severe rotational pattern of the sacrum in relation to the pelvis which was reflected in a pull through the dural membranes from the coccyx to the lower lumbar spine.

The client had come on recommendation of a friend and knew very little about the Bowen Technique. She was therefore somewhat surprised that a treatment so light could be in any way effective, given her medical training. I told her that the treatment tends to release held muscle tissue and can result in stiffness for a few hours as toxins get released from the tissues and work themselves through the lymphatic system. I therefore advised her, as I do with all my clients, to drink plenty of water and to try to keep moving during the day. Although she was somewhat sceptical at this, she agreed to come again next week to continue treatment.

The following week she returned, highly apologetic for her scepticism. She had felt extremely stiff the evening of the first treatment, but by the following morning the stiffness had dissipated. She also said that she felt generally more mobile and that the pain in her back was considerably improved. She was still left with the pain in her left kidney area. After checking that she wasn't suffering from any kidney infection, I proceeded to address the area using specific Bowen techniques. At the end of the session I also suggested various gentle exercises that might help her and made sure that she was lifting correctly in her work.

During the next 2 treatments she made steady progress and by the 4th session (probably the average number of sessions for most Bowen treatments), the kidney pain had gone, her lower

back and sacrum area were much more mobile and pain-free and her periods were much less heavy and painful.

This client now returns from time to time when she has suffered a specific injury and is interested in learning the technique herself to use on her patients.

By John Wilks MA RCST BTAA MIIR ARCM
The Bowen Association UK, PO Box 4358 , DORCHESTER, Dorset, DT2 7XX
UK tel 0700 BOWTECH (0700 269 8324) email; office@bowen-technique.co.uk
web: www.bowen-technique.co.uk

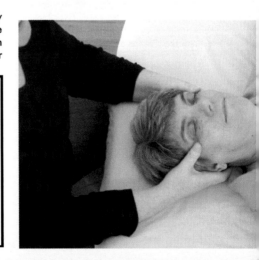

What is Colonic Hydrotherapy?
by Dr Milo Siewert

Colonic Hydrotherapy is an internal bath to help cleanse the colon (large intestine) of poisons, gas, accumulated faecal matter and the mucus deposits. Sterilised equipment is used to flush filtered water through the colon to help expel waste products and compacted deposits.

How does it work?
The colon is the last five feet or so of intestible tube, approximately five feet in length. Food waste enters into the colon from the small intestines in a fluid state and water, minerals and vitamins are then reabsorbed and toxins and other waste materials eliminated through the rectum, therefore if the colon is not functioning correctly, many disorders can result, including constipation, diverticulitis, haemorrhoids, colitis and even bowel cancer. In 1912, the Royal Society of Medicine published a report stating that toxicity in the intestines can be a contributing cause to sleep disorders, mental and physical depression, skin problems, breast cancer, bladder infections, headaches, as well as digestive disorders. The report concluded by saying: "To no other single cause is it possible to attribute one tenth as many various and widely diverse disorders."

What is involved in treatment by Colonic Hydrotherapy?
Filtered water maintained at a carefully regulated temperature is slowly introduced using specialised, sterilised equipment into the rectum. The patients' modesty is maintained at all times and you would usually be given a special gown to wear. The therapist will work progressively around the structure of the colon allowing water to flow in and then release, thereby expelling accumulated toxins and impactions.

The whole process takes about 30 minutes and herbal preparations are sometimes used for specific conditions with regular implants of lactobacillus acidophilus given to assure normalisation of the bowel flora.

What Colonic Hydrotherapy can help?
The Health Education Council, National Advisory Committee on Nutrition Education (September 1983) reported that 85% of the population have slow bowel movements with as many as 40% of the population in the United Kingdom being regularly constipated. When the colon does not function properly, other eliminating organs (e.g., skin, kidneys, lungs and lymph) become overloaded and subsequently they too become affected.

Advocates of Colonic hydrotherapy believe that it will help cleanse the body and take strain off the vital organs. In this way, it may well assist the action of the other therapies or dietary changes. Indeed, the Colonic International Association recommends that Colonic Hydrotherapy "is best used as a complementary technique to other therapies. By improving elimination, response to dietary, homeopathic, herbal, manipulative and other therapies is markedly improved."

 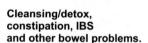

Colour Light Therapy

Our modern style is different from that of our ancient predecessors in one unique way — we live our lives inside. We spend most of our time in closed quarters, be it in our offices, stores, factories, theaters or homes. We place our children into classrooms for the most part of their days, since their early years. We travel in closed vehicles, often with shaded glass to block the sunlight, or commute and shop entirely under ground. We have become concerned over the ozone hole in our atmosphere and its potential harmful consequences, so we readily vacate sunny beaches and often replace them with timed sessions in man-made light-emitting pods.

Ever since the early humans discovered they could make fire at will, the importance of the sunlight was made relative. Nowadays, we routinely substitute daylight with various types of illumination of our own making — candle light, gas light, light from incandescent bulbs or fluorescent tubes. Our lives hence offer minimal exposure to sunlight. When we do venture outside, we continue to shield ourselves from the sole source of life in universe — sunlight — by wearing sunglasses, hats and long sleeves, by applying sunscreens and staying in the shade as much as possible. We consciously choose to live an unnatural life in artificial surroundings. Only a hundred years ago most people spent 75% of their time outside, today the reverse applies. Yet, we were not made for such an existence.

Full spectrum light, at the proper intensity, is essential to the production of Vitamin D in our skin and the metabolism of calcium; the amount of calcium in the system regulates not only our bones, but also our nerves and the thinking process. Nevertheless, we do not readily associate ailments and disorders with our confined lifestyle. Only recently have we identified one - seasonal affective disorder (SAD) - and only in a certain percentage of the population (statistics show that 10 to 25% of North Americans occasionally exhibit symptoms of SAD). Meanwhile, we are faced with myriad conditions, afflictions and diseases for which the Western allopathic medicine offers no compelling explanation or treatment. Chronic anemia, unexplained organ failures, the surge of cancers regardless of age and gender, mental illnesses, depression in all of its modalities and forms — all these signals are diagnosed, recorded and addresses solely as independent events in the lives of individuals (or as statistical data), not as symptoms of a single, planetary condition. Medical doctors always look at ill people to establish what is wrong with them; they do not study the healthy population to understand and define the essence of health.

Naturally, our bodies do not use incandescent or fluorescent devices; to survive, they require the color energy carried by light, which they emit for internal and external communication. Light, when shone through a prism, splits and reveals itself through seven specific colour categories ranging from red, having the longest wavelength, to violet, being the shortest — this is our visible colour spectrum. It is a perfect mirror image of our rainbow. Have you ever wondered why we get so excited, feel like a child again and marvel so much at a rainbow after a spring shower? Perhaps, it is a reflection of our own true inner beauty, our inner source of light. Whether we admit it or not, at a spiritual level, we all feel our inner child within and will chase rainbows until we find our pot of gold outside ourselves, which, of course, doesn't exist. Perhaps we need to discover our rainbow located within each and every one of us at a soul/heart level.

When we find that 'pot of gold' within, we will not need to search anymore. You'll know, it is an all-encompassing, complete 'inner' knowing. Colour can assist you in achieving the unimaginable..

Cosmic Energies

Cosmic Energy is a high level healing energy. It has been brought to us by the Cosmic Energies: high vibrational Beings from the Cosmic Realms, working with us on the Earth Plane.

Cosmic Energy is their vibration, and it is used in a new and different way: Cosmic Energy is not channelled through a human healer, it is received directly from the Cosmic Energies themselves.

All the Cosmic Energy work is done over distance. If a person wishes to receive some Cosmic Energy, a session is prepared for them. They then settle down, wherever they choose, and follow a simple visualisation process - the Cosmic Connection. This connects them to the Cosmic Energies, and allows them to receive the Energy directly. No-one else is involved.

Having made their initial connection to the Energies, they can reconnect whenever they wish. As with anything, the more they connect, the easier the connection becomes, so that soon they can connect to the Cosmic Vibration at any time, and anywhere.

Cosmic Energy can work on the physical level, bringing healing to the physical body, on the mental/emotional level, clearing blocks and bringing clarity, or on the spiritual level, raising an individual's vibration and helping them to evolve. Cosmic Energy can also facilitate transformation, wherever it is needed.

The Cosmic Energies also offer guidance, through channelled sessions - also done over distance. The information is brought through, recorded, and sent to the enquirer, who can listen to it whenever they choose. No physical connection is needed with the Channel.

Many people have now made their Cosmic Connection, and regularly connect to and receive Cosmic Energy. However, the vibration is very fine, and some people are not yet ready for its high frequency.

New processes are being developed where the Cosmic Vibration is combined with other Energy, so that it can be more easily received by those at the beginning of their healing journey. There are now three degrees of the Cosmic Vibration: Earth, Sky and Heaven, each designed for people at different stages on their path. The Earth and Sky vibrations include hands-on sessions as well as distance work.

The pure Cosmic Energy (Heaven) will always be available for those ready to receive it, but the Earth and Sky vibrations will assist and support others as they move towards connecting with the full Energy of the Cosmos. It's quite an experience.

Counselling & Psychotherapy

For some people, these are two separate activities; for others, both words describe the same activity. Either way, they help you to deal with your difficulties or problems more effectively.

Those who differentiate, state that Counselling is short-term and issue-focused in the present, whilst Psychotherapy is long-term and focused on your past. However it is fair to say that at present, there are psychotherapists and counsellors who work both short-term and long-term; there are counsellors and psychotherapists that work in the here and now as well as focusing on your past.

The origins of psychotherapy started with a link to psychoanalytical psychotherapy, which related to the theories put forward by Sigmund Freud and his peers. Counselling's origins stem from a need for non-medicalised therapeutic help.

For many people, now, the two words are used interchangeably. I shall talk about the "therapist" to denote both or either.

The idea behind therapy is for one person (therapist) to help another (client) by listening without judgement, helping the client to gain insights into their problems. This service is offered in a confidential manner and the boundaries of that confidentiality should be clarified at the beginning. This agreement in itself forms the basis for therapy.

Therapists do not usually offer advice; rather they support and enable you to find your own answers through the exploration of your past and present.

Therapy sessions usually last for 50-60 minutes. The length of therapy overall is your decision. It is useful to try a meeting with a therapist to see whether you feel comfortable enough to build a trusting relationship with them, as this is essential to the work. You will generally be required to do more of the talking; the therapist will facilitate the growth in your thinking and awareness.

Do not be afraid to ask questions about their training and experience. They should abide by a particular code of ethics and ideally belong to a professional body that has an independent ethical framework and complaints procedure. Some of the main bodies in the UK include the British Association of Counselling and Psychotherapy (BACP), United Kingdom Council of Psychotherapists (UKCP), The Association for Humanistic Psychology in Britain (AHPB) and British Association of Psychotherapists (BAP). There are of course, more.

Therapy can be helpful for men, women and young people from all backgrounds. It can be useful for a wide variety of life situations, including work, personal, health, and so on. When you want or need greater clarity on something; when you want or need support from someone outside of your immediate family and friends; when you need to make decisions; when you need or want to understand yourself and or others better, therapy can help. Therapy can also be very helpful for expanding your range of choices; exploring inner conflicts; development of the self; and indeed how you relate with the world.

Some therapists only work through the talking medium; others work through art, toys, movement, visualisations, singing etc, in addition to talking. The one you choose depends on your personal preference and different things will work at different times, for different people. There is therapy available for individuals as well as couples and for families. Sometimes it can feel difficult to talk about your personal issues to a stranger; but if you persevere, and develop a relationship based on trust, it can be very effective.

Some people go to therapy for specific things they need help with, like career issues, relationships, stress, depression, anxiety, communication difficulties, loss or bereavement, and low self-esteem to name a few. But some people go to therapy when things seem generally difficult but the reason(s) for this seem unclear and they feel lost in their lives. Others go to learn about or develop themselves. You do not have to be "ill" to seek therapeutic help.
Indu Khurana Therapist, Life Coach and Consultant

Sexual Minority Therapy, sometimes known as gay affirmative therapy is not a separate theoretical model of psychotherapy; it can span all models i.e. psychoanalytic, gestalt, person-centred, cognitive behavioural etc. Sexual Minority Therapy challenges the traditional view that same sex desire and fixed homosexual identities are pathological. This approach regards homophobia, as opposed to homosexuality as a likely cause of psychological distress in gay, lesbian and bisexual people. It was only in 1993 that the World Health Organisation removed homosexuality from the list of diseases. Homosexuality is still considered by some therapists to be inferior to heterosexuality. Sexual Minority Therapists also work with people around gender issues, especially with people who are not happy with or confused by their gender presentation. Some of these people may be in the process of transition and seeking support for gender reassignment, others may have been born intersex (with both male and female sexual organs), others again looking to find a place and feel comfortable in the continuum of gender identities.

Sexual Minority Therapists will not pre-judge someone's sexual or gender preferences. They are familiar with working with a range of sexual and gender orientations and identities. If you are concerned or confused about sexual or gender issues, then seek out an experienced therapist who works in a sexuality affirmative manner. The Directory of Pink Therapists (www.pinktherapy.com) lists over 200 such therapists around the UK.

Indu Khurana runs a personal change management practice in East London, providing

Counselling & Psychotherapy

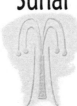

Craniosacral therapists recognise health as an active principle. This health is the expression of life - an inhoront ordering force, a natural internal intelligence. Craniosacral Therapy is a subtle and profound healing form which assists this natural bodily intelligence.

It is clear that a living human organism is immensely complex and requires an enormous amount of internal organisation. Craniosacral Therapy helps nurture these internal ordering principles. It helps increase physical vitality and well-being, not only effecting structural change, but also having much wider implications e.g. improving interpersonal relationships, managing more appropriately etc. Dr William Sutherland, an American osteopath, discovered intrinsic movements of the bones of the skull around the turn of the century. His further research revealed different rhythmic tidal motions in the body. These movements, which can be measured with delicate scientific instruments, are a direct expression of the health of the system. As research continued it became apparent that these movements are inextricably linked with not only physical health but also mental and emotional health. Palpation of these tide- like motions allows Craniosacral therapists to facilitate change in areas of restriction. This restriction of movement corresponds to a lack of the capacity of the life force to express its self-healing. This absence of health may result in disease or a sense of something missing or numbness.

The whole of our life history is held in our physical form. An integral part of this work is the patient's developing awareness of how their story is held and how it unfolds. We are a unit of life function and this is completely respected in Craniosacral Therapy.

The work can address issues in whatever way the client wishes; physical aches and pains, acute and chronic disease, emotional or psychological disturbances, or simply developing well-being, health and vitality.

Craniosacral Therapy is so gentle that it is suitable for babies, children, and the elderly, as well as adults; and also in fragile or acutely painful conditions. As a whole body therapy, treatment may aid almost every condition, raising the vitality and enabling the body's own self-healing process to be utilised.

The following is a list of some of the common conditions treated;

Arthritis	Insomnia
Asthma	Lethargy
Autism	Menstrual, PMS
Back pain	Migraine
Birth trauma	Post-operative
Bronchitis	
Problems during/after pregnancy	
Cancer	Reintegration
Cerebral Palsy	Fall or injury
Colic	Sciatica
Depression	Sinusitis
Digestive problems	Spinal curvatures
Drug withdrawal	Sports injuries
Dyslexia	Stress related
Exhaustion	
Tinnitus and middle ear problems	
Frozen shoulder	TMJ (jaw) disorders
Hormonal imbalances	Visual disturbances
Hyperactivity	Whiplash injuries
Immune system disorders	

The work can be profoundly relaxing, exhilarating, deeply moving or involve a resolution of old material. Sometimes the benefits are not immediately noticeable but become obvious on returning to a familiar environment. Sessions are usually between 40 - 60 minutes in total.

Craniosacral Therapy and Babies
For a Craniosacral therapist, treating young babies and their mothers is undoubtedly one of the most rewarding experiences. Babies (especially new-borns) tend to respond very quickly and effectively to treatment, especially for conditions like colic and sleeplessness. Just as a seedling can be nurtured with the smallest amount of physical guidance to grow into a healthy plant, so a baby, by the gentlest of encouragement, can be helped to release the stresses and trauma of the birth process and so avoid possible physical and psychological trauma later in life.

The compressive forces experienced during birth as a result of the passage through the pelvis and the tight fit in the birth canal can cause imbalance in a baby's system, even in natural and apparently problem-free births. Many babies experience difficulties through the use of Ventouse extraction, forceps or Caesarean deliveries. Every type of birth has its own compressive patterns on a baby's

Craniosacral Therapy

body, especially its head, and Craniosacral therapy can go a long way to easing these patterns through the therapist's light touch and receptive listening .

'Valentina definitely has healing hands she leaves you with a sense of well being and deep relaxation and has the ability to get rid of nagging complaintsî Heather Farmbrough, London.
îValentinaís hands hover over the body and encourage the channels to wake up. Energy literally courses through'. Tania Shillam, London.
Testimonials by Valentina Candiani

Crystal Healing

We have come to view Crystal Healing as a relatively new therapy, but the healing properties of Crystals and Gemstones have been known to man since time immemorial. They were used as talismans in Biblical times, as power symbols by the ancient Egyptians and Mayans, and by the Native American and Aboriginal Medicine Men for healing and Shamanic Journeys. Plato also made reference to them within the Atlantean Temples in his famous dialologues. In India, the relationship between Gemstones and astrology is part of everyday life, and in China there has been an ongoing relationship with the extraordinary properties of Jade since the beginning of the Dynasties. In recent times, through much research and study, we have re-learnt how the energies of crystals can help us with our health and healing, on the physical, mental and emotional levels, as well aiding us in our spiritual development.

Crystal Healing, as a therapy, can take many forms, from Gem Elixirs, which we take internally, to the more well know art of laying-on-of stones. When you visit a Crystal Therapist, after the initial consultation, you will be asked to relax on a comfortable therapy couch, and be covered with warm blankets or towels, whilst listening to soft relaxing music. While you lie there, drifting into a state of deep relaxation, the healer will carefully choose specific stones and gems appropriate to your needs, and then gently place them on and around your body, focusing often on the energy centres (or Chakras).

All matter has a vibratory energy, including crystals and people. What makes a crystal unique from all other matter is the fact that its vibration is constant, while our vibrations fluctuate all the time. During times of disease and disharmony our vibrations may be lower than usual, so by carefully selecting a crystal that matches our own frequency in balance and harmony, we can gently raise that level of vibration back to its health and vibrant level. Different gemstones and crystals have different vibratory rates. For example, Calcite has a lower, gentler frequency than, say, Sapphire, which is very high. The therapist learns how to tune into these different frequencies, and can thereby choose the precise and perfect crystals required by the client. It is not unusual for up to 60 gemstones and crystals to be used within a healing session, as the interaction of the different crystal frequencies and energies can bring about a very subtle, yet powerful changes.

Crystal Healing is a beautiful yet profound experience, but crystals are beings that can enhance every aspect of our lives. Wearing a Tiger Eye in a piece of jewellery can really help to boost your self-confidence, or carrying a small Snow Quartz will certainly help to create an air of peace and harmony around you, so try it if you know you are going into a stressful situation and feel the difference it can make as it interacts with your auric field.

Crystal healing is one of those rare arts that can blend well with almost every other therapy or technique available. Think of a therapy that you are familiar with, such as Aromatherapy or Reflexology, and try to imagine ways in which the crystal energies could enhance them. For example, by placing a small tumbled amethyst crystal in the oil blend in Aromatherapy, you can enhance the relaxing, therapeutic properties of Lavender oil, or by adding a piece of citrine you can create a lively, invigorating blend, supporting, perhaps, Rosemary or Ginger.

Anna was experiencing severe lower back pain following a total hip replacement. She was concerned by the amount of analgesia she required and unhappy because her life was so restricted. After three treatments the pain had lessened considerably and Anna was taking very little analgesia. Having worked initially on the physical level I then began to address Anna's emotional pain. She was feeling happier more relaxed and peaceful and could not believe the change in her energy and mobility. **By Jayne Taylor Crystal Therapist**

Energy Field Therapy

This therapy is an approach to healthcare which originated in China and has only recently come to this country. It produces outstanding results. A subtle but powerful treatment, it is based on the clearance of blockages from the body's energy field. Our physical body is surrounded and permeated by an electrical field, the natural flow of which is essential to our health.

The flow can become blocked through emotional trauma, disease or accident and this results in a disruption of energy to the major organs of the body. As a result our physical and emotional health is affected, with the body becoming sluggish, fatigued and, eventually, diseased.

How is the therapy given?

The therapist is trained to be sensitive to the patient's energy field, using the hands to 'scan' that field, without touching the body, locating and clearing areas of blockage. The patient is treated either standing or lying down as appropriate and remains clothed.

The treatment is given for up to 3/4 hour a day over four consecutive days. During this time the flow of energy within and around the body is freed and enhanced; this 'kick-starts' the body's natural ability to self-heal. In the weeks that follow many changes will occur, leading to an increased sense of well-being and improved health.

How many courses of treatment are needed?

Although for some patients one course is sufficient, most will need at least one follow-up treatment; these are given at six-weekly intervals. It must be remembered that this is not a 'quick fix' but a deep approach which goes to the root of the problem and, consequently, can take time in cases of serious illness.

What conditions can be treated?

Energy Field Therapy is used to treat any condition; it has helped people with, for example: Multiple Sclerosis; Cancer; M.E.; Cerebral Palsy; Rheumatoid Arthritis; Head Injuries and Central Nervous System damage.

It has also produced excellent results with conditions such as: Migraine; Menstrual Irregularity; Sciatica; Allergies; Depression; Irritable Bowel Syndrome, Panic Attacks; Circulation Problems and Asthma.

The therapy is very effective in helping slow-healing fractures and in reducing recovery time after surgery or any injury. It also helps reduce the level of tension in the body generally, and can help physical pain of unknown origin (e.g. chronic back pain where there is no recognized cause). It is an excellent aid to dealing with stress.

Who can be treated?

Anyone of any age and level of mobility. Babies and children respond especially well to Energy Field Therapy, whether they are seriously ill, or simply going through a difficult period (e.g. after a traumatic birth, or suffering because of bullying, parental divorce, etc.) Animals are also very responsive, even in cases where other methods of treatment have been unsuccessful.

Mary suffered from migraine attacks and after the consultation. I used non-contact Energy Field Therapy to establish where the energy imbalances were. During the next three days I corrected the imbalances using a combination of Energy Field Therapy techniques and Reiki. After this treatment the migraine was cleared up. By Keith Harmon

What can Feng Shui do for You?
(Science helps sort out the fact from the fiction)

How would you like to make a positive difference to your health, income or relationships?
Feng Shui has helped thousands of people with these areas and many more.
'How', I hear you cry! Well let's take a closer look.....

For those who are perhaps a little sceptical about the benefits of Feng Shui, modern science can provide a wealth of research to back up the simple fact that our environments do substantially affect us.

Colour Therapy?
The use of colour is very important in Feng Shui and a substantial body of scientific research highlighting the significant impact that colour has on our mood, now backs what Feng Shui has been saying for centuries.
Red represents fire in Feng Shui. It has been shown to be very stimulating to the brain and overuse can lead to excitability, anxiety, migraines, impatience and irritability. For this reason red should be treated with care, (like fire) and used in smaller amounts to add zest where appropriate.
Green represents the Tree element and has been shown to stimulate creativity, optimism and ideas as well as bone growth and good posture!
By contrast the Blue end of the spectrum particularly violet at its far extreme, representing the water element, has a very calming effect on us and is particularly good for restful sleep. Earth tones (principally yellow, terracotta, pink and peach) provide supporting, nurturing influences and can also be quite restful as long as they are not too vivid. Yellow has been shown to enhance sociability and communication and reduce introspection and can therefore be a useful asset to reduce bickering. Yellow flowers are a classic Feng Shui cure for ongoing arguments.

A Picture paints a thousand words.......
There's also mounting evidence to show that artwork can affect our mood and even our physical well-being.
The last impression we have as we close our eyes should be of a clear, tranquil space with positive, harmonious images around us. Artwork and ornaments should be peaceful and non-confrontational: the last thing you want to see before going to sleep is a picture of a bullfight or a poster of 'Terminator II'.

I suggest that you take along hard look at all artwork I your home (or office) and ask yourself 'do these images reflect the essence of what I'd like my life to be about? If not change them.
Of course the specific placement of certain pictures is very important but we don't have time to go into that here.

Science has also shown many other aspects of our buildings can affect us. These include....
the types of materials used in the structure, decoration and contents of the home; (eg sensitivity to toxic paints, furniture and cleaning chemicals). If re-decorating try using natural paints, carpets and other materials rather than synthetic ones. Once installed, try cleaning with simple water (or at least the less toxic cleaners)

Electro-magnetic frequencies (EMF) from your
mains supply and appliances. Try moving all electrical equipment at least 3 feet away from you in bed. Install batteries into your alarm clock or

Feng Shui

place it on the other side of the room which make it a better alarm clock anyway!; try pulling your bed 6 inches away from the wall to see if you feel better (walls often give off the highest electrical fields due to the cables they carry or dampness)

Plants: There is no better way to enliven and freshen the interior than through the use of plants. This is perhaps the most obvious way of bringing nature directly into a building to create harmony. Plants have many positive attributes:

a: They help charge the atmosphere with negative ions which have a positive effect on our physical and mental health.

b: They enhance the supply of oxygen in our surroundings.

c: They help soak up electo-magnetic radiation from computers and other equipment.

d: They enliven a space through colour and beauty.

e. NASA recently discovered that certain plants absorb toxic gases from the air

The type of energy coming from the Earth beneath the home:
Dowsing can be used to detect earth energies that are harmful and beds should then be moved to a safer place.
......The list goes on.
Most of the so-called 'esoteric' side of Feng Shui can also be explained through the recent advancements in Quantum Physics, but that's another story!

Julie's career was slow and she had been single for six years. She and her mother Brigitte said 'no matter how positively they thought nothing flowed.' The Feng Shui gave them a path to deal with their issues. Julie now has a partner and her career has blossomed. **By Sarah Higbid.**

After years of bad luck, using Feng Shui principles, I discovered which areas of my home were in disharmony. Once I balanced these, my life began to improve dramatically. Things got so good I gave up a 30-year career to become a Feng Shui Consultant. Read why on my web-site: **www.planetpakua.co.uk**

"From the day we moved his bed to the suggested place, my son has slept through every night. He is also a lot happier and remarks how much he enjoys being in his room now. The space clearing made the entire house feel somehow warmer and calmer. Even my husband, who at first thought me entirely mad for considering Feng Shui, had to admit that it has worked. We are thrilled." **L McIlheney, London N16 (The Feng Shui Agency Limited.)**

Goal to change the flat from a single to a shared living and work space. "Suggestions for optimizing energy-flow through colour and space-utilization proved simple and effective. The flat has transformed into a spacious light area where it is possible to dance, practice Tai Chi and meditation. Students, clients and friends all love it." **Amravati of Amravati Heaven on Earth**

Planet Pa Kua, 74 Chigwell Road, London, E18 1NN. Tel: 020 85188686 See main advertisement under Products and Services on page 74.

Flower & Vibrational Essenses

Even quite knowledgeable people often confuse Flower or Gem Essences with other products such as essential oils, aromatherapy oils or herbal extracts. Flower Essences hold the vibrational energy signature of the flower, plant or mineral from which they have been made. This non physical energy code is transferred by sunlight to natural spring water made potent and strengthened by the intention of the essence maker. No less it becomes the voice of the plant, in a bottle that whispers a message from the natural world to our inner ear. An essence will talk directly to the heart and supply answers and guidance, waking us to the acceptable alternatives that will guide us through difficulties.

There is nothing new about Essences, They have been made for centuries, a practice that has been quietly passed through family lines until early in the 20th Century. This was when Dr Bach with his work on stereotypes and patterns of illness, channeled the energies of plants to produce a range of 38 remedies that formed the focus of Flower Essences for the best part of that century. The most famous of Dr. Bach essences is the combination essence known as 'Rescue Remedy' which has enjoyed widespread acceptance and popularity. The needs of society today are a lot more complex than when Dr Bach produced his 12 healers. With the 21st Century we are finding that rapid shifts and changes play a major part in disturbing the mental emotional and spiritual balance we seek and that amidst the fast and constant change the answers we seek need to come from a pure source. The producers of Flower Essences have responded to the new energies with a great deal of vision and insight. There are new essences emerging daily;

Some made by individual producers, others are large scale but all are well developed to professional standards that are an important part of product regulation. These new essences are not necessarily single flower remedies. More and more Essences are seen to be combinations of flowers, minerals, trees, animals plants, astrological events and environmental features collectively the Essences of today are becoming a most powerful factor for support of emotional, mental & spiritual change in our time. The choices are from the entire planet and include Australian Bush Flower, Alaskan Room Sprays, Tree Essences, Animal Essences, Indigo Child Essences, Chakra Colour Essences, Rainbow Essences tuned to the body energy system and Himalayan Flower Essences.

An essence in its simplest form is made by floating flowers of a plant on a glass of fresh spring water in sunlight for several hours. During that undisturbed time the wisdom and knowledge of the plant and place where it is made is passed from the petals into the water. The water is filtered and stored in a preserving solution usually brandy from which it is further dispensed into individual dropper bottles use. The essence maker's knowledge of the nature of the plant enables suggestions of guidance for the uses of the essence but this does not prevent a user selecting a suitable essence through their own intuition and inner choice. The beauty of using vibrational essences is that they are self empowering and do not place the user into inferior role. The normal way of taking essences is to place 3 drops in water and drink 2 or 3 times a day until results are evident. Alternative to taking the essences by mouth, the essences can be sprayed into the room, rubbed onto the skin or hair, dropped into bath water. They can be placed on it clothing, hair or absorbed into the air around the body. Vibrational essences are finding their way into well known mainstream products as ways to improve beauty, products such as hand and face creams, shower gels, lip balms and as mentioned before room sprays. Terry Webber. Rainbow Essences, www. rainbow-essences.co.uk

Herbal Therapy

Herbal Medicine is a system of healing that uses plants as medicine and is common to all cultures and traditions. It is the oldest system of medicine in the world and is still the primary form of health care for much of the world's population. Both traditional Herbal Medicine and modern drugs have a role to play in our health care and Qualified Herbal Practitioners can treat a wide range of complaints with herbal medicine.

The Herbalist's Approach

Medical herbalists are trained in the same diagnostic skills as doctors but take a holistic approach to illness. The underlying cause of the illness is sought and, once identified, it is this that is treated, rather than the symptoms alone.

Specific herbal remedies are used for their affinity with certain body systems to restore the balance of the body enabling it to mobilise it's own healing abilities.

What Happens at a Consultation?

A consultation with a Medical Herbalist usually lasts up to an hour. In this time the herbalist asks lots of questions to enable them to build up a picture of the patient and their general health. They take a full case history, also discussing past medical history, diet, lifestyle, stress levels and family medical history. It may be necessary to take the patient's blood pressure or arrange for other tests to be done. At the end of the consultation an individual treatment plan is discussed, including herbal remedies, dietary and lifestyle changes, and relevant nutritional supplements.

It is usual to have about three to five follow-up consultations with a herbalist to assess the patient's progress, followed by regular checkups every 3 to 6 months.

The Herbal Prescription

Herbal medicines are prescribed for patients using individual combinations of herbs. Herbal prescriptions are usually given in the form of a liquid tincture and taken in 5ml doses two or three times daily. In addition, herbal teas, ointments, creams and tablets may also be prescribed.

What Conditions Can Herbal Medicine Treat?

Most of the problems that you take to your GP can be treated with Herbal Medicine. A Qualified Medical Herbalist will have studied orthodox medicine as well as plant medicine and will be able to diagnose and treat a wide range of health problems. Arthritis; migraine and other headaches; skin complaints including acne, eczema and psoriasis; menopausal symptoms and other gynaecological problems (e.g. PMS, fertility issues and polycystic ovary syndrome); digestive disorders such as IBS, stomach ulcers or inflammatory bowel disease; depression and stress are some of the health problems that can be successfully treated. Herbal Medicine is safe to use at all ages from the elderly to very young children, who respond especially well to the gentle approach of herbal medicine.

Are there any side effects?

Because herbalists use whole plant extracts and not isolated extracts of plants, as many drugs are, side effects are rare and only usually occur with misuse of herbal medicine or in people that are sensitive to particular plant constituents. If you are allergic to any medications or foods, please ask your herbalist for advice.

How To Identify A Qualified Medical Herbalist?

Members of the National Institute of Medical Herbalists (N.I.M.H) or the College of Practitioners of Phytotherapy (CPP) adhere to a strict code of ethics and have undergone an intensive 4-year course in Herbal Medicine including 500 hours of supervised clinical training. They also study botany, clinical methods, diagnosis, physiology, pharmacology, and herbal therapeutics during their training.

Members of these professional bodies will have the letters M.N.I.M.H or M.C.P.P after their name and this identifies them as fully qualified and insured Medical Herbalists.

Homoeopathy is an extremely popular, accessible and versatile form of alternative therapy that has gained an increasingly high profile over the last decade or so. However, homoeopathic medicine is no newcomer to the health scene, since its history goes back approximately two hundred years to the ground-breaking work of the conventional physician Samuel Hahnemann. Since then, it has established itself as an effective form of alternative treatment on a global basis, practised by professional homoeopaths and conventional doctors alike.

Homoeopathy is one of the most genuinely holistic forms of therapy available, since it is the aim of the homoeopath to support each patient to an optimum experience of health through the prescription of the most appropriate homoeopathic remedy. In order to arrive at this point, it is necessary for the practitioner to find out as much about each individual patient as possible through sensitive and detailed questioning. As a result of the in-depth nature of the case-taking, the first homoeopathic consultation should take roughly an hour to an hour and a half. During this time questions are likely to be asked about the patient's experience of health on all levels including history of previous illness, current health problems, stress load, sleep pattern, energy levels, digestive problems, the presence of any allergies, and a detailed family history. Rest assured, this shouldn't feel like an inquisition since once a patient realises that they can relax and have plenty of time to explore their problems in detail, things tend to flow easily and naturally. In fact, many patients find this experience of making sense of the development of their problems a therapeutic experience in itself.

Once the homoeopath has obtained enough information to gain an insight into the patient as an individual, it is time to do a case analysis when the relevant homoeopathic prescription can be selected. This may be done by using custom-made homoeopathic software, or a number of text books. The object of the exercise is to find the single homoeopathic remedy that matches the symptoms of the patient most closely on mental, emotional, and physical levels. When the most appropriate remedy is selected and taken, it appears to act as a catalyst, giving the self-balancing and self-curative potential of the body the kick start it needs in order to get on with the job efficiently. As a result, when improvement takes place it should

not be limited to the piecemeal disappearance of symptoms. Instead, there should be an appreciable improvement in energy levels, emotional and mental balance and a general increase in a sense of well-being. As a result, homoeopathy may be seen as a system of healing which is aimed at positive health promotion, rather than being limited to disease management.

Homoeopaths have an especially important role to play in helping patients who suffer from a range of chronic conditions such as skin disorders (including eczema and psoriasis), stress- related problems including migraines, tension headaches and anxiety, hay fever, menstrual problems such as premenstrual syndrome, and a tendency to recurrent infections. By Beth MacEoin

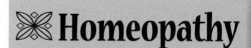

Homeopathy

Healing by trance state (hypnosis) is one of the oldest phenomena known to man and is found, in one form or another, in virtually every culture, worldwide. It could also be legitimately described as the original psychological therapy and somewhat more contentiously, as the basis for many of the more recent styles of psychological intervention.

Although the trance state has been known for thousands of years, the term "hypnosis" (from the Greek "hypnos", meaning "sleep") was only coined in 1842 by Dr James Braid and remains a somewhat less than accurate description of the experience, as the hypnotic state is, in most respects, entirely dissimilar to sleep.

What is Hypnosis?

At our current level of knowledge, no one is entirely certain although a reasonable definition would be that: Hypnosis is a state of mind, enhanced by (although not exclusively) mental and physical relaxation, in which our subconscious is able to communicate with our conscious mind. It may be better to define "hypnosis" by what it does rather than what it is and in this regard, it is widely accepted as a most excellent method by which we may access our inner potential. The state of mind referred to may be brought about either by oneself, unaided (self-hypnosis) or with the help of another person. If this other person is a trained professional, who utilises the resultant state of mind to encourage beneficial change to occur, the process is referred to as "Hypnotherapy".

People are sometimes concerned that they will "lose control" in hypnosis but this is not the case. Regardless of how deeply people may go in hypnosis and however passive they may appear to be, they actually remain in full control of the situation. They are fully able to talk if they wish to (or not, as the case may be) and can stand up and leave the room at any time. Neither can a hypnotised person be made to do anything against their usual ethical or moral judgement or religious belief. It is likely that the notion of a loss of control stems from most people's misconception of stage hypnosis, wherein participants are apparently made to perform all manner of foolish acts. Participation in a stage act is an entirely voluntary process (thus "permission" is already given to the hypnotist) and that there can be no such volunteer who is unaware of exactly what they are letting themselves in for!

Who can be hypnotised?

The answer to this question is undoubtedly "virtually everyone". This claim must, however, be qualified by the observation that some are more readily hypnotisable than others and that it will also depend upon one's willingness to be hypnotised at the time. This willingness will itself depend upon a number of factors, not least of which will be the strength of the person's particular need and their trust and confidence in the therapist concerned. A corollary to this question is "What level of trance is required in order to achieve a beneficial outcome?" Although there remains some disagreement over the answer, most researchers concur that the actual level (or depth) of trance obtained does not relate to the beneficial results that might be obtained. In practice, this means that even where a person feels that they have not been hypnotised, given time (and this is a very important factor), the desired outcome of therapy might yet materialise. This matter of time is especially important in our current society, which has, in many respects, been coerced into believing that gratification of every desire should be instantaneous. Hypnotherapy can be extraordinarily effective but it is not magic. If the right ingredients are present, however, much can be accomplished.

Hypnotherapy

Inderjit Bans dip. GHR reg.Create a more fulfilling life)
Hypnotherapist, Counsellor, Reiki healer, relaxation
therapist, phobias, confidence building, panic attacks,
depression, stop smoking. etc. Tel/fax 0208 574 2552
mob. 07950 445728   e-mail mannsaffer@aol.com

Patrick Browning MA LLM FCA DCH DHP. Behavioural
change (eating, sleeping, smoking, phobias etc),
stress, motivation, self-confidence, skin and gastro-
intestinal disorders. Group relaxation classes. www.
browning-hypnosis.co.uk   0207 2290098

Professional Hypnotherapy Training Eligibility to join
professional registers, obtain professional indemnity
insurance. Tuition by highly experienced hands on
therapists, payment options:
0845 456 9537 – www.health-concern.com

A Good Way Forward
Tanya Colley BA(Hons) GHR Reg. LNCP
Eating Problems, Phobias, Stress and Anxiety, Weight
Loss, Smoking, Confidence Issues
www.agoodwayforward.co.uk   0208 682 3861

Ciaran Kelly Dip HypPsych(UK)
Hypnotherapy and Psychotherapy Practice in Ealing.
Healthy Body, Mind and Spirit. For a free 15min
consultation contact info@ciaranbkelly.co.uk or
phone 07854731056

Sow seeds for a change! Give up ciggies; shed excess
baggage; release phobic butterflies. Keith Ealey,
Registered Hypnotherapist, Psychotherapist,
Karuna Reiki® Master. London, West-End. Tel:
07710 356448

Carole Murray. Classes and private sessions available
in North London for mothers who would like a
shorter, easier, more comfortable birth. HypnoBirthing
lessens the need for chemical analgesia as couples
are taught self-hypnosis techniques to achieve deep
relaxation. 35 Avondale Road, Finchley, London
Tel/Fax: 020 8922 5652
Email: carolemurray@ntlworld.com

HYPNOTHERAPY FOR ME

Adrian Dodd DHyp, BSCH (Assoc)

Member of the
British Council of Clinical
Hypnosis

Phone (020) 8926 2138
Mobile 07949 213 207

Based in Chingford

www.hypnotherapyforme.com

★ Stop Smoking ★ Weight and Eating
Problems ★ Stress Management
★ Pain Control ★ Anxiety ★ Phobias
★ Exam Nerves ★ General Health
★ Nail Biting and Blushing
★ Personal Performance
★ Public Speaking and Shyness

Derek Ross
GHR Registered Practitioner

Hypnotherapy, Regression and specialist in the use
of hypnosis to treat a variety of medical conditions.
Relief from back pain and stress or weight loss
and 'stop smoking'. Centrally located in the
heart of the City of London.

City Clinic - 62 Aldgate High Street
London EC3N 1BD - Tel: 020 7481 8666
www.ross-wildman.co.uk
Email: derek@ross-wildman.co.uk
Mobile: 07766 542054

Margaret Sinclair
BSc.(Co.Hons). MSc. DCH. DHP. MNCH(Lic). GQHP

Clinical Hypnotherapist

Raynes Park, London. SW20 9DY
Telephone: 020 8395 6766
E-mail: margaret_hypno@hotmail.com

Iridology

What is Iridology?

Iridology is a true analytical and diagnostic tool which mainly concerns itself with the iris (the colored part of the eye), the sclera (white part of the eye) and the pupil, to reveal what goes on inside our bodies.

The iris is made of thousands of individual fibers and different layers. Each single fiber is connected to nerve endings which in turn is connected to the brain. As we develop, the iris stalk extends these nerve endings outwards, providing a God-given, exposed, microchip of information. An experienced practitioner can instantly see what is going on inside the body. As soon as there are changes in the body, there will be relevant changes in the iris. On the other hand we are also born with genetic weaknesses, which again are shown clearly in the iris, and might or might not come into manifestation at some point in life, depending on lifestyle and nutrition. Being aware of those gives us the advantage to support the weaker organ parts in advance and thus being able to prevent illness in the first place.

The only thing that is not visible in the iris, are operations - as due to the anesthetic all nerves are temporarily paralyzed, so no information can be transmitted to the brain.

Iridology owes a lot to various medical doctors, mainly in Germany, Russia and America, who have done extensive research, in comparing their findings with autobiopsies and therefor verifying their first impressions. In 1000 BC the Chaldens of Babylonia were carving depictions of the iris topography into stone slabs, along with the reflex zones to human anatomy.

In general there are 3 main constitutions:
The blue or lymphatic eye
The brown or haematogenic eye
And the mixed iris which is a combination of the above two, which we call biliary.
All in all there are 25 constitutions which derive form the 3 main types

A qualified practitioner, for example, will be able to spot any misalignment of the spine, to the exact vertebrae, which still astounds many osteopaths. One can survey the entire digestive tract, see whether one is fully digesting nutrients or whether certain enzymes are missing, thus causing us problems with various foods; note any blockages or disease of the digestive tract etc. even worm nests, which are not as unusual as one might want to think.

For so many years we have relied on doctors to treat our ailments that we have forgotten to take some responsibility towards our own health. We just go with our symptoms and leave with a prescription and hope it will do the trick. Sometimes it does and sometimes it does not. Why is that?
In Iridology we know that one symptom might have many different root causes and we rarely use the same treatment on two people coming with the same problem. We look at the whole system and only then it can become clear what needs attention.

By Sonja Scherndl M.H., M.R.N.I., M.G.N.I.
Full Member of the Guild of Naturopathic Iridologists International

Kinesiology

Kinesiology is rapidly gaining in popularity as a powerful but gentle way of helping people regain their health and achieve their potential. People consult a kinesiologist for many different reasons. They may want help with physical problems, including eczema, asthma, migraine, arthritis, hay fever, allergies, M.E., menopausal problems, menstrual problems, tiredness and IBS. They may have been through a whole range of medical tests and have no diagnosis for their symptoms. Their symptoms may be controlled by drugs, but they seek help because they are worried about taking drugs for the rest of their lives. They may be emotionally stressed and distressed and want help with depression, anxiety, panic attacks, lack of self-confidence, etc. Faced with shops full of nutritional supplements claiming to have the answer, the bewildered shopper may seek advice from a kinesiologist on exactly which supplements are best for them. Sports people may seek the help of a kinesiologist to improve their performance. Children with dyslexia, ADDH and other problems can be helped too. An accident victim suffering pain and emotional trauma, or a person who cannot see the way forward may follow up a recommendation and consult the nearest kinesiologist.

The basic tool – kinesiology or muscle testing – allows the practitioner to access information about the client that neither the practitioner nor the client may know at a conscious level. Kinesiology is in a unique position amongst alternative and complementary therapies. It can be practiced as a complete discipline in its own right with its own protocols and therapeutic techniques, or else it can be used as a tool to provide practitioners in other disciplines (such as aromatherapy, chiropractic, Bowen therapy and homeopathy) with additional information and insights.

Muscle testing is a painless procedure involving the practitioner applying gentle pressure to specific parts of the body (often arms and legs) to test the response of the underlying muscle. The particular part of the body involved is placed in a specific position, in order, as far as possible, to isolate the muscle that is being tested. The muscle will either easily be able to resist the pressure from the practitioner or will give way, at least slightly. The Kinesiologist uses this response to access information about what is happening and what is needed. Because of the inter-relationship between muscles, meridians and body systems,

this information can apply not only to the muscle being tested but also give valuable information about other imbalances within the body and the necessary procedures to correct them. If, for example, a muscle tests spongy or unlocks in the presence of a food it may mean that the person is allergic to that food. A stressful thought will also result in an unlocked response from an associated muscle.

There are various branches of kinesiology. All use the basic muscle-testing skills. Each kinesiology very much reflects the interests and personality of its developer, but all kinesiologists are united by a fundamental belief and experience that each of us has an innate understanding of what is needed to become truly healthy. This information is at an other-than-conscious level and not easily accessible via the conscious mind, but it is accessible through the tool of muscle testing.

Jane Thurnell-Read is author of the book Health Kinesiology.
www.lifeworkpotential.com

E arrived with severe Irritable Bowel Syndrome, extreme headaches, knee problems and back pain. Treatment 1 lasted 30 minutes at her insistence as she was so sensitive to treatments. The result was that the IBS cleared. She came running into my treatment room smiling to me the following week saying she couldn't believe it for he first time in her life she had had no diarreha for a week. Treatment 2 we found the root cause of the headaches was the emotional scarring left by a broken skull which had happened in a childhood fall 45 years ago.

Treatment 3 The knee problem was sorted out by pinpointing a badly fitting crown. I recommended the Kinesiology dentist who muscle tests ensuring all fillers and glues are suitable for the client. Lower back pain is due to dehydration and simply drinking 2 litres a day of plain, still, room temperature water clears so many problems and gives one a wonderful complexion too. When we get into stressful situations the body dehydrates causing pain and many problems. I have many stories like this and it is wonderful to see people feeling better. Let me share my joy with you. **By Barbara Harvey of Barnes London**

Sue came in a distressed state following a medical diagnosis of M.E for which no real prospect of improvement had been given. Using Kinisiology to find the body's immediate requirements we were able to bring calm to the situation. In subsequent sessions a variety of Kinesiology techniques and associated therapies were used to allow Sue to take back control of her life. She is now able to live her life to the full using skills developed to maintain wellbeing. **By Terry Shubrook Kinesiologist**

"Ellisa, aged 9, came to see me because for many years she had been unable to eat her food without vomiting and feeling dreadful. She was also afraid of the dark and couldn't sleep in her own room. This meant she was unable to stay with friends for fear of becoming ill and sleepovers were a no no. After three treatments Ellisa can now eat what she wants, is not afraid of the dark so sleepovers with her friends have become an enjoyable part of her life." **By Linda Hodges Registered Kinesiologist**

Lastone Therapy

LaStone Therapy was introduced in 1993 by Mary Nelson, from Arizona. Since that day its popularity has grown throughout the world and is available in major destination spas through to individual private practitioners. Mary was a massage therapist wanting a way to be able to work more deeply without causing further damage to her joints and muscles. She is also very spiritual and it was this combination that led her to the stones.

To start the treatment you will receive energy work to enable you to receive the treatment at its best. It is this work and the alternating temperature that sets LaStone apart from the more recent 'stone' treatments on the market. The combination of the energy work and the chemical response within the body during a LaStone treatment demonstrates the flexibility and the balance of the treatment.

The stones

Not only do the stones deliver the temperature, they also pass on their own personal energy. The stones come from the earth and they are hundreds of thousands of years old. They have the resonance of the earth and this passes to the client, energising or relaxing. The stones are in pairs in order to make the strokes feel just as balanced and smooth as the therapists hands are.

The further beauty of this treatment is that it can extend the life of a therapist by many years. Most practitioners of body work suffer at one time or another from injury, strained muscles and aching joints. LaStone takes the pressure off the joints, allows the therapist to work deeply without tiredness and actually gives the therapist a treatment at the same time as the clients – receiving the temperature from the stones throughout the treatment.

Thermotherapy

The use of hot stones is what intrigues the clients, the feeling of being warm and relaxed appeals to everyone. The idea of the chilled stones is not always as appealing, but it is the cold that does the deepest work. The cold is the most effective and if the therapist applies it correctly and sympathetically then the client won't actually notice the temperature, they will just feel the difference from before to after.

The client's response

LaStone is an all round treatment, suited to those looking for stress release, relaxation and balancing or those needing a thorough work out on their body to be able to move away from injury and into total fitness.

Most of us have areas we would like to change in our lives and ambitions we want to fulfil but we are often unsure where to start.

Successful life coaching creates a special rapport between coach and client which helps you overcome barriers and achieve goals in your personal and professional life. Coaches use a range of interpersonal skills; they are trained to listen, ask insightful and sometimes challenging questions to identify your ambitions and dreams. Coaching does not dwell on the past but deals with the here and now and developing your existing strengths. It focuses on your well being and enables you to move your life forward in a positive way.

Coaching facilitates learning, development and personal performance, helping you make the right decisions and changes to take you to where you want to be.   It will help you realise your potential and overcome the blocks and inhibitions that so often hold us back.

Coaching brings confidence

Talking to a caring and trained coach who offers you completely non-judgmental support gives you a powerful tool to find the confidence to change and improve your life.

The coaching profession covers various sectors, including business and corporate but life coaches usually work with individuals to help them in both their personal and professional lives.

Typically areas covered by personal coaching include career development and career change, personal relationships, fitness and weight loss, managing stress, improving work/life balance, goal setting and motivation.

Coaching is about change

Coaching is all about change for the better. It's a supportive and practical process that is results oriented. Clients are encouraged to think for themselves and discover the best path forward.

Coaching allows people the space and time to take a step back and look at a situation from a new and fresh perspective. The coach also helps build self belief and the client's commitment and motivation to ensure that desired goals are achieved.

How coaching works

Coaching can be given either in person or over the phone - sessions can last between 30 and 60 minutes. Generally, an initial free consultation is offered to find out the area or issue you want to address, build a good rapport and fix a timetable for action.

Remember coaching is not a quick fix and to succeed it requires a high level of commitment. Although you can benefit from just one session, the coaching relationship is usually based on weekly sessions over several months.

Some goals may be everyday, some life changing - they are all important to the coach because they are about you, the possibility of change and the opportunity to enjoy a fresh outlook on life.

With new self-belief, you will be able to release untapped potential and build a more exciting life plan for the months and years ahead.

Ann, a teacher in her thirties felt lonely and depressed following a break-up with her partner and found she no longer enjoyed her job.
By Carole Deighton

I asked Ann to think of creative ways to make school lessons more challenging nd set her the goal of finding ways to meet new friends. She joined a gym and yoga class and with increased confidence she now enjoys her social life. She feels more fulfilled at work and has recently been promoted. **Carole Deighton – Life Coach**

My life wasn't tragically going wrong and it wasn't the most successful. I was comfortable, kind of monotonus living. Deep down I knew there was more to me, desperate for a change and challenge; I took up the opportunity of coaching. Out of this revelation was born my passion to coach others and help to make a difference- a treasure I needed to share. Whether it's business career, personal or wellbeing why not create your life the way you want it. **Neelam- Designer Life**

Qualified professional coach whose London based practice focuses on personal development and career change. Telephone: 020 8809 0796 email: carole.deighton@btconnect.com

When you feel under the weather - tired all the time, prone to colds or skin problems - what do you do? Take a daily vitamin supplement, get more rest and try to eat a healthier diet, perhaps? Sounds sensible, but you could be better off having Manual Lymphatic Drainage therapy. It is the most effective way to boost the lymphatic system, one of the body's most powerful weapons against illness and a vital component of your immune system.

Manual Lymphatic Drainage is a very gentle skin movement technique. No oils or creams are used, (but may be administered on completion of the treatment) steaming blankets are a definite contra-indication and no pain should be experienced if being treated by a skilled and qualified therapist.

About 50% of the population suffers from a weakened lymphatic system, and trouble with it can trigger a whole range of seemingly unrelated complaints, including bronchitis, laryngitis, ear and eye problems, asthma, eczema, sinus trouble and cystitis.

The human lymphatic system is mainly ignored, and more often abused, despite the fact that it works round the clock to remove cellular debris and foreign bodies, reduce excess fluids, fight infection and repair damage throughout the body. By boosting your lymph, you will not only have fewer colds and be less susceptible to illness; you will also have clearer skin and brighter eyes. It may even reduce cellulite.

Alongside the system of arteries, veins and capillaries that transports blood from your heart to your cells and back again, there is a separate - but connected - network of lymphatic channels. The fluid that passes along these channels, called lymph, both delivers antibodies, that fight infection, and removes toxins from the body's tissues, transporting them to various lymph nodes (in the groin, behind the knees, in the armpits and under the chin - among others) where they are filtered out and destroyed. When this system becomes blocked by an infection or overloaded by excessive toxins, problems can occur. Depending on what area of the body is blocked, the tissues react in different ways - which is why symptoms can vary from acne to cystitis.

Luke had a broken wrist and twisted shoulder, 5 years previously. When the shoulder pain returned, he was prescribed painkillers. Sleeping was difficult, he walked stiffly and feared any kind of physical treatment. With 1 session, he could sleep. With 3, he could lift his arm to 90 degrees without pain. With 5, he booked in to see his regular therapist and was recovered soon after.
By Tanga Okondo-Totterdell

MLD sessions cost from £30. There are nearly 200 MLD UK practitioners in the UK.

Massage

The message of massage is universal: you can use your hands to help literally anyone. Massage is one of the simplest ways to achieve and maintain good health, to show someone that you care, to comfort and soothe.

Massage is probably one of the oldest healing therapies known to man, it is an extension of basic instinct seen in animals and humans alike: apes groom each other, animals lick their wounds, humans rub away their aches and pains. The basis of massage is touch- the most fundamental of human needs; in fact, touch is so important that if it is absent or withdrawn it can lead to all sorts of problems, ranging from failure to thrive in babies, irritability and bad behaviour in children, and depression in adults.

There is evidence of massage in most ancient and more recent cultures. The fact that it has survived for so long and evolved into different branches simply reinforces its reputation as a universal panacea.

Massage relaxes, stimulates, comforts, soothes, shows caring and empathy, relieves stress, anxiety and depression, alleviates pain, reduces symptoms of minor illnesses, improves emotional and physical well-being. The list goes on and on.

The important thing about massage is that anybody can do it, anybody can have it done, there are no side effects, it can be adapted to individual needs, and most importantly it makes the receiver and the giver feel good. In the frantic materialistic and technological age in which we now live, many people have lost touch with their inner feelings and in particular how to feel good about themselves.

Throughout history and all over the world, we use our hands to promote healing. Although it is safe to say that the use of massage preceded written history it is more difficult to say when it was first mentioned. The Ancient Egyptians used massage extensively for health and beauty as can be seen from tomb paintings dating back to 3000 BB. Recorded comments about massage were made by the Greek physician Hippocrates, who noted in the 5th century BC that "Rubbing can bind a joint that is too loose and Loosen a joint that is too ridged...hard rubbing binds, much rubbing causes parts to waste, and moderate rubbing makes them grow". One of the earliest references to massage in a written form can be found in a book on traditional Chinese medicine dating from the 3rd century BC. The Yellow Emperor's Classic of Internal Medicine informs us that massage as a form of medical treatment was specific to the people of the central region of China, who "suffer from complete paralysis and chills and fevers..... most fittingly treated with breathing exercises, massage of the skin and flesh, and exercises of the hands and feet".

In India, massage plays an important part in Ayurvedic medicine dating back over 3,000 years. The Ayur-Veda (Art of Life), a sacred Hindi book written about 1860 BC, describes shampooing (massage) to reduce fatigue and promote well-being: "Rise early, bathe, wash the mouth, anoint the body, submit to friction and shampoo and then exercise" Avicenna the great Persian physician (980-1037 AD) wrote; "The object of massage is to disperse the effete matters formed in the muscles and not expelled by exercise. Massage removes fatigue; such as friction is soft and gentle and best done with oil" The relevance of this statement is seen today in the increasing number of athletes who use massage as part of their fitness regimes.

Massage is now one of the fastest growing complementary therapies. Trained massage therapists now work in hospitals, hospices, psychiatric units, neurodisability centres, schools for children and adults with learning difficulties, special care baby units, intensive care units, old peoples homes, and complementary medicine centers. They may be attached to sports centres, dance centres, professional football, rugby and cycling clubs, offices and health clubs.

There is increasing medical evidence to show the great benefit of massage and data from hundreds of studies highlight the effectiveness of massage therapy for maintaining health and decreasing chronic illness. For example it has been found that pain-syndromes have been decreased by massage; stress and depression has been shown to be alleviated by massage; autoimmune conditions such as asthma and dermatitis are reduced possibly because negative immune function is reduced and there is a reduction in stress hormones.

In one study with hospital staff they were given 10 minute massage during their lunch break. The massage not only led to decreased stress but the subjects were more alert and performed math problems both quicker and more accurately.

Yet with all this evidence to show the benefit of touch we are still hesitant we are still hesitant about touching each other and that is one of the wonderful things about massage, it is simply an extension of the basic human need to touch and be touched. Massage is formalized touch and therefore gives you a licence to touch: and thus remove the taboos of touching and allow people to touch in a positive formalized way.

Remedial massage (Soft tissue massage)

Remedial massage uses several specialised techniques to locate and repair damage and support and speed up the body's own repair mechanisms. During a remedial massage session, the original area of pain or immobility is traced back to the original causes as far as possible. The first session will be question and answer to obtain an overall view of your health generally both current and historic, and about any injuries you may had. You will then be offered a general relaxing massage, to release tension in muscles, increase blood and lymph circulation, speed the removal of waste products in the muscle tissue, and regain flexibility in soft tissue. There will be specific tests for trigger points, scar tissue and muscular imbalance, to assess whether the pain is due to soft tissue damage or muscular imbalance and if so, how and why it has originally arisen. Treatment will be given as appropriate to improve any imbalances discovered, to reduce pain etc, and increase muscle mobility. You will be given advice on any exercises or specific massage you can do yourself. During subsequent sessions treatment will be tailored to treating areas of damage or restriction and restoring balance and flexibility to the system, diminishing the likelihood of further problems.

Indian Head Massage (Champissage)

Indian Head Massage is guaranteed to lift you out of the hustle and bustle of everyday life. The therapy, which has been practised on the Indian sub-continent for over a thousand years, is absolutely ideal for counteracting 21st century stress. This special head massage can be enjoyed in the office, at home, in a clinic or in fact anywhere there is a chair. It is wonderfully relaxing and does not require the need to undress or the use of oils. Indian Head Massage provides relief from tension

headaches, migraine, eyestrain and muscular aches and pains in the neck and shoulder areas. It relieves stiffness in the neck and helps to improve concentration while diminishing many stress-related symptoms. It is excellent for insomnia; helps to encourage hair growth; soothes, comforts and also re-balances your energy flow. It's wonderful for promoting a deep sense of peace, calm and tranquillity.

The head, neck and shoulders - all energy centres where tension is most likely to accumulate are gently, firmly and rhythmically massaged until the pressure begins simply to melt away. A session normally takes 30 minutes. There's a specially adapted, shorter version for busy office workers. A special word to all those who depend on computers in the office or at home: Indian Head Massage is the ideal way to release all tension, strains and frustrations that can build up after hours in front of a screen. In fact, you can depend on Indian Head Massage to effectively ease that feeling of pressure which can so easily increase throughout the day. This de-stressing massage, received before an important meeting, interview or exam, leaves you feeling relaxed yet alert and able to produce your best work without feeling tense or tired. And it's superb for imparting a feeling of well-being before any social occasion.

The practice of meditation can simply be seen as using a set of tools which promote a state of health, peace and balance in life. Contrary to common belief, it is does not have to be linked to religious beliefs, nor is it a difficult skill to master. It does not require any special aptitude. Meditation is a simple and natural process. It is easily mastered, with guidance, by people of all ages and all temperaments. If you can think, you can meditate – it's as simple as that.

As living organisms we are naturally predisposed to be in a state of balance and wellbeing. This is because every cell of our bodies is capable of producing endorphins, the 'feel-good' biochemicals which create the physical feeling of happiness. Many of us no longer connect readily with this state of mind as we have progressively become distanced from our true nature. Meditation can empower an individual to restore the balance.

The mind-body connection

Using meditation techniques can trigger the production of endorphins in the system to dissolve tension and strengthen the immune system. Moreover, we can channel and guide this 'energy' through the system at will. It is possible to do this because energy follows thought. Simply by thinking about a particular part of your body creates a neural pathway connecting your mind and body together. By directing positive pleasurable sensations around your body, you subtly influence the state of your physiology. This is not imagination but fact; neuropeptides, the chemicals that carry information around the body, respond to thought quite automatically. This, in a nutshell, is the mind-body connection.

How meditation works

We all have stresses which reside in our system resulting from past traumas, accidents, illnesses, and sadness; even negative personality traits and attitude can stifle the system.
These stresses, lodged far deeper than normal sleep can resolve, are what prevent us from accessing the pure source of our vitality directly. This results in less clarity of thought and an inability to attain fulfilment in life. In a very real sense meditation is a tool for effective action and a means for positive self-expression by using the natural tendency of the mind to gain deep rest. In this state the body is able to dissolve the stresses in a very simple and unchallenging way;

What are the benefits?

Meditation can be of benefit to all. Scientific studies have shown that meditation techniques can: improve memory and intellectual performance, reduce anxiety and stress, enhance sleep quality, improve relationships, help you cope with life's demands and adapt to change, strengthen health, immunity and resilience, safely release past trauma, relieve stress-related disorders, reduce blood pressure, assist recovery from addiction.

How easy is meditation?

Meditation techniques are simple to learn with guidance and, once learnt, will be yours for the rest of your life. They will help you through the difficult times and enhance the good times. Regular practise is not as difficult as you may think, even though we all have busy lives and the environment in which we live is often not as quiet or peaceful as we would like. However, this is no bar to meditation. By simply learning to 'let go' we can use those times of day which might be called 'empty'. For instance a commuter on train or plane can use the time spent travelling to work to creatively recharge the batteries.

Laura suffered from depression and anxiety during a difficult divorce settlement. The ensuing life changes as a single parent with financial insecurity brought further stress and she developed hypertension. Joining a meditation group she found moral support as well as relaxation. Through regular practise she has gained a sense of balance, strength and general acceptance. Her confidence and awareness in everyday life has increased. **By Linda Hall**

Metamorphic Technique

The Metamorphic Technique is a simple tool that enables us to move from feelings of limitation towards accessing more of our potential. In short, it helps us to help ourselves.

During a session, the practitioner uses a light touch on the feet, hands and head. A safe, relaxing space is provided where you can ëjust beí. There is no need to take a case history. Some people may wish to talk, while others enjoy taking time out. A session usually lasts from 30 to 60 minutes.

Each of us has natural abilities that we can connect with, given the right environment. The practitioner provides that space. The Technique offers a unique approach to handling personal issues, whether they are physical, mental or emotional. These matters will influence how we are able to respond to events in everyday life.

People are often drawn to the technique in times of difficulty, career changes, moving house, divorce, bereavement or illness or because they feel at a crossroads or ìstuckî in their lives. Many find they cope better in these periods of transition. Some may wish to make deep inner changes without having to analyse the past, others find that in times of stress they are able to deal with situations more effectively. It allows them to deal with emotional issues and make deep inner changes without having to discuss their problems or delve into their past.

As the name suggests, the Metamorphic Technique is concerned with change and transformation, which can occur on a number of levels ñ physical, mental, emotional and behavioural.

While practitioners cannot predict the outcome, as each personís life force is unique, the majority of people who have experienced the Technique do report benefits ñ it is unusual for the personís energy not to act in some beneficial way.

On a physical level, people come with a variety of conditions from cancer to chronic fatigue. The Technique does not seek to address these conditions or their symptoms; however in many cases people find that symptoms diminish over time, or that they respond better to other treatment they have been following.

The Metamorphic Technique has been used a great deal in work with physical and mental disabilities, as well as in schools for children with learning difficulties, in hospitals, in prisons, and in providing an environment for people to overcome addictions, eating disorders and stress-related conditions. It is also used by midwives and pregnant women, who can experience an easier pregnancy and birth.

The technique is safe for everyone, it is self-empowering and it enables you to steer your own path. It can be received on its own or alongside conventional or complementary approaches. It can be safely used by everyone, including ill or dying people. The Metamorphic Technique is easy to learn and is accessible to everyone.

For more information see our website: www. metamorphicassociation.org.uk.

Neuro muscular transmission (NMT) is a simple technique using gentle touch or no direct contact. It is a process of reprogramming designed to bring about fundamental change on a physical, emotional and psychological level. The aim of the treatment is to restore the mind and body as far as possible to its original state by accessing the internal communication systems. The NMT practitioner acts as a facilitator in this process.

A comprehensive consultation prior to treatment will determine the approach to be taken, physical or emotional. You remain clothed throughout in a comfortable position lying, sitting, even standing. The therapist is guided intuitively to lay hands on your body. This can be confusing for it may not always correspond to the site of your pain! Your brain registers the contact through the nervous system and a process of reprogramming begins. It is a highly complex process. The brain assesses the problem in relation to its 'original blueprint'. The 'positional release' mechanism will start a process of reversal to resolve the problem. This is a natural process we use every time we are in pain. We move quite naturally into a 'position of ease'

and our pain disappears. The brain registers this and releases the tension from the corresponding muscles. This process will be repeated many times during a session. The therapist's role is to follow these movements and hold the body in position while the brain registers the change. The treatment may include the whole body or specific areas. No two treatments are ever the same. If no change occurs - no matter how small - within 2-3 treatments, the therapist must question - is this the right treatment for this problem? or is there an emotional / psychological problem creating physical symptoms?

During the session you may feel:
- very relaxed, even drift off to sleep
- tenderness in certain areas
- soft tissue moving although there is little to see on the surface
- a sensation of air or water flowing through the body

The experiences are many and varied. Your therapist would have a comprehensive list.
The process has three different stages:
1. Resolution of a problem which may be acute

Nutritional Therapy

Food is a powerful medicine that has a huge impact on the biochemical processes of your body. There is now an enormous amount of scientific knowledge showing the effects of food and nutrients on treating illness and preventing diseases. Research has shown that good nutrition can have an impact on a wide variety of problems, including female hormone imbalances, infertility, weight problems, children's illnesses, skin conditions, bowel disorders and prevention of degenerative illnesses such as cancer, heart disease, osteoporosis, arthritis etc...

Nutritional therapy is not just about eating well. It is also about correcting any vitamin or mineral deficiencies, improving digestive function (because you are what you eat, but also what you are able to absorb), balancing hormones naturally, and eliminating toxins and waste products.

Using nutrition as a form of treatment works quite differently from conventional medicine. The first aim is to work on the symptoms by addressing the underlying cause of the problem. The next stage – and here's the big difference – is to work on prevention so that the problem does not recur.

By ensuring that you have good levels of the correct vitamins and minerals and that you eat well, you are supplying your body with the tools to heal itself, correct any imbalances and restore good health.

This is where nutritional therapy is so different from conventional medicine (also known as 'allopathic medicine'). For example, if you were suffering from an infection, you would probably be prescribed antibiotics to kill off the bacteria. In nutritional therapy, the aim would be to stimulate and strengthen your immune system, so that your body can kill off the infection on its own.

What's the difference? The conventional approach leaves you weaker, as antibiotics tend to disrupt your system, killing off healthy bacteria that is part of the defence mechanism. Furthermore, your body has not 'learned' to fight off infection on its own, and chances are that the exact same problem will occur again. By using the nutritional approach you will encourage your body to do the work, leaving it stronger and more able to address similar illness in the future.

As well as looking at what you eat, vitamin and mineral supplements can be extremely useful. You may wonder why you might need them, particularly if you have a good diet. Unfortunately, the well-balanced diet is a myth. You simply do not get all the nutrients you need from your food. This was confirmed from a National Food Survey conducted in 1995, which found that the average person in Britain is grossly deficient in 6 out of the 8 vitamins and minerals surveyed and less than 1 in 10 people receive the RDA (Recommended Daily Allowance) for zinc, an extremely important mineral.

We have, as a society, begun to eat far too many processed, convenience and refined foods that have been stripped of essential nutrients during the manufacturing process. For example, 80 percent of zinc is removed from wheat during the milling process to ensure that a loaf of bread (for instance) has a longer shelf life.

Furthermore if you, like a large proportion of the population, have been dieting for a number of years – either restricting your food intake, or trying different diets, diet drinks or pills – you are more than likely to be deficient in a number of important vitamins and minerals.

The other reason why it is important to use supplements is that you want to achieve positive health benefits in as short a space of time as possible. Certain nutrients, depending on your problem, will help to speed up this process because they can help you to detoxify, improve digestion and absorption and strengthen your immune system as well as balancing hormones and helping you to lose weight.

But it is important to remember that supplements are just what their name suggests – supplemental, or 'extra'. They are not a substitute for healthy food and a well-balanced diet. You cannot eat junk food and take nutritional supplements and hope to stay healthy. **Wishing you good health. Marilyn Glenville PhD**

Amanda C. Tyrrell
Diet and Nutrition Consultant
ITEC Diet and Nutrition
ITEC Anatomy and Physiology
Mobile: 07932 001079
Email: amandatyrrell@yahoo.co.uk

The birth of a baby is a moment of great strength and joy. Today's expectant parents can now choose how their newborn will come into the world. They can choose a hospital or a midwife at home. They can decide what kind of setting they want during labour and delivery. They can opt for a natural birthing process or one with pain management. They can also choose who will be present to support the mother-to-be and to celebrate the birth.

Homeopathy for parents-to-be and babies

From pre-conception to post-natal period, homeopathy is the ideal medicine system. Made from minute amounts of active substance, remedies are safe to use at a time when conventional drugs are best avoided.

Homeopathy promotes good health in both parents prior to conception, thus enhancing the health and vitality of your baby. It can relieve bothersome symptoms in pregnancy, from morning sickness to piles, and rebalance the emotional swings common at this time.

Remedies can help with pain relief in labour and facilitate the natural birth process. They are useful in treating post-natal problems, from mastitis to depression, and offer a safe alternative to conventional drugs for common problems in babies, such as colic, constipation and teething. By Grazia Gatti RSHom, Tel: 0208 5332656, grazia@gatti.freeserve.co.uk

HypnoBirthing is as much as philosophy as it is a technique. It is a rewarding, relaxing, stress-free method of birthing that is based on the belief that when a mother is properly prepared for birthing physically, mentally, and spiritually, she can experience the joy of birthing her baby in an easier, more comfortable manner. The method is based on the belief that severe discomfort does not need to be a natural accompaniment of labour.

The aim of the programme is to build confidence in the mother and for her to have confidence in her own ability to birth her baby. The philosophy of the Hypnobirthing programme is to educate the mother about the wonders of her body, to eliminate fear, as well as teach her the skills to work with the birthing process rather than fight against it. In many cases it is fear that undermines the mothers confidence in herself. One of the tasks of the Hypnobirthing practitioner is to help the mother change her belief that the experience of

childbirth is fearful and to help her tap into her own deep resources to develop confidence in herself, to dismantle the Fear - Tension - Pain Syndrome. The work is about "changing old beliefs, learning new meanings." In my experience, many mothers need to be freed of the negative images of birth, which they receive through the media, stories from mothers, grandmothers and friends, to understand and experience the belief that birth can be natural and beautiful.

In the HypnoBirthing classes, the couples are helped to understand that previous negative knowledge and experiences have a detrimental influence on the present birthing experience. This birth can be different! The mother is introduced to techniques of controlled breathing and relaxation as keys to her success. The scene is also set for deepening techniques through visualizations and imagery. The important issue of pre and postnatal bonding and welcoming their baby is also covered.

Rebirthing

What is it?

Rebirthing or Integrated Breathwork is a wonderful tool for self-exploration. It is a simple, gentle yet powerful technique which allows you to access, release and integrate memories, emotions and patterns stored in your body, mind and soul that hinder you to live your full potential, physically, emotionally and mentally.

How is it done?

After discussing your particular needs with your Rebirther' the session itself is done sitting up or lying down. Having been guided through a relaxation sequence, you consciously connect your breathing so that there are no pauses between the inhale and the exhale. The breathing is relaxed, yet full. Slowly you will be guided to find your own rhythm, probably slightly faster and fuller than you are used to. Every breathing session has its own cycle which includes an activation phase (20 to 40 minutes depending on the individual), an expression phase where we work with the material that surfaces and an integration phase. The length of a "breathe" is generally one to one and a half hours, a full session usually lasts for two hours.

How does it work?

The breath is the bridge between the conscious and the subconscious. You can control your breathing consciously (e.g. pranayama breathing exercises) but if you don't think about your breathing even for the whole day, you still are breathing. Rebirthing works on the principle that there is a direct connection between mental Gerd Lange Page 2 and physical well being and the openness of the breathing. Relaxing and releasing the breath dissolves tension in the body and mind.

KASIA SIKORA

*Rebirthing
Breathwork*

Mob: 0781 384 7475
H: 0207 8130245

Physiological explanation

Through breathing continuously without break, your body becomes mom oxygenated than usual, which changes the CO_2 level in your brain. You enter a self -induced trance state where memories, pictures or emotions can come up to the surface to be reviewed, released and integrated. The power of Rebirthing is that in this state you are the experienced and the observer of a past incident at the same time, and therefore able to release or re-interpret what happened then from a new and conscious angle.

Holistic explanation

Through conscious connected breathing you accumulate life force (prana, chi, ki) which starts to move freely through your body (experienced as tingling, energy rushes or waves). This loosens up stored blockages held in your four-body energy system (physical, emotional, mental and spiritual), thus working on all four levels at the same time. Therefore possible experiences can be manifold and may vary every time. The spectrum ranges from physical sensations of pain or pleasure to release of emotions (sadness, anger etc.), realisations of dysfunctional thought patterns or new thought connections and insights, and deeply spiritual or energetic experiences or any combination thereof.

The Rebirther

The Rebirther is your guide on the journey. He/she will skillfully maneuver you through the surfacing material, witness and validate your experiences, help you to stay present and to maintain your mental clarity. To integrate what has come up a skilled Rebirther will use various psychotherapeutic integration tools ranging from Counselling, Family Dynamics, the Inner Child, psychic surgery, past life etc. The Rebirther's most needed qualities, besides being professionally highly trained and experienced, are unconditional personal regard and to be nonjudgmental and compassionate.

'I felt energy flowing through my body and saw beautiful colours. I had a strong sense of well being and love. I finished refreshed and confident: all the muddle and confusion was gone. It gave me the courage to start changing my life.' Clare, company director By Kasia Sikora

Reconnective Healing

Truth is sometimes stranger than fiction. It's astounding how much our world has changed. Not just advancements in technology or medicine. Our entire understanding of humanity and the universe is evolving.

Spirituality, alternative medicine and holistic practices are suddenly household words. Near death experiences, the afterlife, angels, and miracles are today's most popular film and television themes. Spirituality-based self-help books top the bestseller charts. We're captivated by what exists beyond the physical. Might this shift be what's brought us our most unusual discovery yet: access to a new level of healing and evolution so powerful, so real, that it's attracting international crossover audiences from mainstream medicine to the metaphysical community, and everyone in between?

As explained in his international bestseller (12 languages), The Reconnection: Heal Others, Heal Yourself, these new frequencies of healing – yes, you heard me, new – are incomprehensible in their magnitude. Known as Reconnective Healing Frequencies, they were first brought through by Dr. Eric Pearl in Los Angeles. A chiropractor at the time, his patients suddenly began reporting miraculous healings from cancers, AIDS-related diseases, cerebral palsy and more, without him physically touching them. He merely held his hands near them!

Baffled, top doctors and medical researchers worldwide are studying these new frequencies in an attempt to understand just how they work, and what makes them so much stronger, more palpable and dramatically more effective than Reiki, Johrei, Jin Shin, Qi Gong or any healing "technique" yet encountered. The most current studies are at the University of Arizona by Gary Schwartz, PhD, professor of medicine, neurology, surgery, psychology and psychiatry, with Harvard and Yale backgrounds. The University of Miami School of Medicine plans to launch its own clinical study, says Mark O'Connell, MD, internal medicine specialist and Senior Associate Dean for Medical Education. This definitely rattled my construct of how the body works – how disease works, adds O'Connell.

Scientists offer that these frequencies are possibly available on the planet for the very first time.

It's as if we suddenly have access to a more comprehensive bandwidth or range of healing frequencies that encompasses everything we've ever had access to in the way of "energy" healing, known or unknown, and more. Far beyond energy healing, Reconnective Healing functions as a catalyst producing benefits at every conceivable level, possibly restructuring our DNA, allowing us to reconnect to our "perfect blueprint" of health. Fascinatingly, each of us appears to be able to carry these frequencies – once we come into contact with them. We do, however, have to come into contact with them first. Although medicine remains in the dark as to how Reconnective Healing actually works, studies reveal that these frequencies are transmittable, showing changes in seminar attendees' abilities after Pearl's weekend workshops.

As with medicine – as with anything – Pearl the first to acknowledge that there are no promises or guarantees. Three people can present with the same set of symptoms, the same diagnosis, and receive three different sets of results. The outcome is determined by the intelligence of the universe. Yes, people get up out of wheelchairs. Not all of them – some of them. Yet enough of them to make an impact, to demonstrate that this is something very different, something very real. Beyond faith. Beyond religion. Yet in harmony with God, Love and Universe.

Healing at this level of Reconnection goes beyond symptom-based treatment or therapy. Healing is about balance. Through bringing balance, symptoms merely fall off, no longer serving any purpose because the cause of the health challenge no longer exists. This, Pearl explains, is the essence of true healing.

+1.323.960.0012 US   +44.(0)1754.899870 UK

Reconnective Healing

'Saw gridlines of light across the body. Many people have gaps so light can travel through' (SB). 'At beginning lots of laughing. Felt inside of body dancing spiral movement' (WP). 'Felt connected to the universe' (TK). 'Had past life experiences. Many thanks Mo' (TM). 'What you gave was a real gift' (DB). **By Mo Razak.**

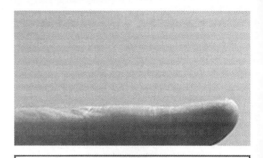

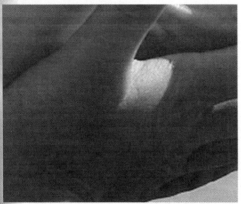

Reflexology is a specific pressure technique applied to the feet or hands where all the internal body structures and organs are mapped or mirrored in miniature. It is a simple non-invasive treatment which helps the body to maintain a delicate balance between the nine systems. (Skeletal, Muscular, Vascular, Neurological, Respiratory, Digestive, Endocrine, Urinary, and Reproductive). All these systems work together in harmony and unison to keep the body in a state of good health.

No one knows exactly how Reflexology works although many theories exist. Most Reflexologists subscribe to the theory that the body is divided into ten longitudinal zones (or energy pathways). These zones are lines running the entire length of the body; five on each side of the median line (an imaginary line running from the crown of the head to between the feet)

The zones extend into the feet which are also divided into ten zones, five on each foot. The foot zones are located with number one on the first toe (big toe) counting to number five on the little toe. These lines are repeated, running down the arm to the fingers. On the hands number one zone or channel runs to the thumb and number five to the little finger.

Energy chi or qi (pronounced chee) flows through each zone/channel. When the energy flow is blocked by congestion disorder and even disease can occur. When the therapist treats a reflex point the main aim is to enhance the energy flow encouraging the body to heal itself and the systems to work again in unison. Another benefit of the therapy is to break down tiny waste deposits (known as crystals) that can sometimes be found at reflex points (especially joints) and encourage their removal through the normal elimination process.

On each foot and hand are found areas known as reflex points corresponding to each gland and structure in the body.

The hands and feet have the same reflex zones and points; however there is belief that treatment of the feet gives better therapeutic results than does treatment of the hands. Whilst all therapists believe in the benefits of the treatment there are some who believe that because of the mobility

of the hand the reflex points are not so clearly defined and are more difficult to locate. Yet another school of thought is that because the total body weight passes through the feet and as the feet are more protected from the elements the energy channels and reflex points are more sensitive to touch.

Medical Dr's William Fitzgerald and Edwin Bowers are generally acknowledged as the forefathers of modern reflexology. Fitzgerald was head of the Ear Nose and Throat unit at St Francis Hospital, Hartford, Connecticut. As early as 1917 he discovered that pressure on the hands and/or feet produced pain relief in distant parts of the body and the condition causing the pain was also relieved.

Fitzgerald went on to confirm that the parts of the body which had such reflex relationships lay within longitudinal zones or channels. He traced ten of these zone lines through the body and called his therapy 'Zone Therapy'.

Reflexology

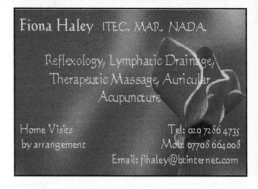

Reiki

The word Reiki, pronounced RAY-KEY, is Japanese and can be translated as, 'healing for body and mind'. Reiki is the name used for the Usui system in the world today.

The practice of Reiki is an original method of healing developed in Japan in the 1920's by Mikao Usui. It was devised by him as part of a system that can be used for oneself, this was its main purpose, or for the healing of others.

He wrote," Our Reiki is something absolutely original. Through it, the human body will first be made healthy and then peace of mind and joy of life will be increased. Today we need improvements in our lives so that we can free our human beings from illness and emotional suffering."

This gift, to use Reiki for yourself and find the peace and relaxation which is then possible in life, is what makes Reiki unique among all other forms of healing therapy available at the present time, which concentrate on the healing of others.

There are many types of Reiki available for those who wish to either receive treatments or to be shown how to use it for themselves. Although at first glance this may cause confusion, it is worth bearing in mind that all styles of Reiki use the same energy the only difference will lie in the method used.

To understand how these differences came about, we need to look at where Reiki came from. Although it was known that Reiki came from Japan, the western form originated in America and then spread to Europe and beyond. The changes that some of the teachers made to the way Reiki was used in America led to the differing styles of Reiki available today.

For a long time it was thought that Reiki was no longer used in Japan, but some western teachers are in contact with those who had been students of Mikao Usui and a clearer picture is beginning to emerge.

So, What is Reiki ?
Mikao Usui in his manual said that it was intuitive. It goes where it is most needed or flows in response to the needs of the person receiving it.
It works on all levels, both physical and emotional; Reiki energises and heals the body. Research has shown that it can speed up wound healing, lower

blood pressure, reduce stress and help in the management of pain. It can be used by itself or alongside any other healthcare and can help to minimise the side effects of conventional medical treatments.

Reiki is not a religion, nor is it a new age practice. No belief system is needed to benefit from receiving Reiki; all you need is a wish to be healed.

If a treatment is offered by a Reiki practitioner, the person being treated simply sits or lies fully clothed and the practitioner places their hands on or near to the body. The person receiving the treatment usually feels deep calmness and relaxation. They may also feel warmth, cold or tingling or other sensations. Each person will have different needs and so your experience will be an individual one.

Energy is said to surround us and flow through our bodies along energy pathways- sometimes called meridians. If the energy is blocked the body's own natural healing will be blocked as well. By the placing of hands on or above the body, the Reiki practitioner allows the energy to flow into the

Reiki

person needing it. That person's body then uses this energy to clear any blockages as it flows.

This is how a Reiki treatment works.

The unique thing about Reiki is that it can be learnt by anyone to use for themselves.

This will relax your mind and body, relieve stress and help to maintain your health in both body and mind.

By learning to be more relaxed our minds become steadier and less agitated. By being less agitated we may find peace within ourselves.

How do you choose a practitioner or a Teacher?

The best way may be to speak to as many as you need to find one who you can feel comfortable with, or attend a free talk.

Unfortunately at this moment in time, although there are a number of organisations who represent differing styles of Reiki, there is no legislation that controls the practice of Reiki to the public.

Reiki organisations will be coming together to discuss how to ensure that the best practice of Reiki will be provided for the public and to see if there is a possibility of setting up a Regulatory Body to ensure high standards in both the practice and Teaching of Reiki.

This means building on the initial groundwork covered by the UK Reiki Federation who have worked with the Foundation for Integrated Health and with government bodies like the Sector Skills Council.

In the meantime, many Reiki organisations have lists of practitioners and Teachers. They can be contacted and will be able to let you know what standards they expect their members to have and to be able to tell you of practitioners and teachers in your area.

Client A came to me to receive Reiki treatments for a number of health problems. He suffered from chronic asthma, RSI in his left knee causing stiffness and muscular pain in his right leg. He received 6 treatments over a period of 3 weeks.

Client A experienced continued improvement in mobility in his left knee and right leg, pain relief

and a significant improvement in his ability to breathe freely throughout the course of treatments. After the last treatment he could walk pain-free and found breathing much easier than before.

An important factor in the improvement of my client's healing process, particularly his asthma, was a shift in his mental and emotional response to life's stresses and strains. Reiki is a holistic treatment nurturing body, mind and soul. By Sue Routner – A1 Healing

'Rejuvanessence - The Angel's Touch' is a unique holistic therapy - sometimes known as the 'Angel's Touch' or the 'Fingertip Facelift' - which uses precise, and gentle fingertip massage to release tension in the 91 muscles of the face, neck, skull and shoulders.

It softens and lifts the face, creating a younger, healthier, happier appearance. It also works on the connective tissue to make it more elastic and flexible, enabling the skin to gain back the texture and look of younger days.

But Rejuvanessence is far more than just a beauty treatment. Working on the meridian lines and acupuncture points, the technique restores the natural flow of energy, balancing and revitalising the body and spirit.

The many benefits of Rejuvanessence include:
Reduction of fine lines and wrinkles
Improvement in skin tone
Eradication of the signs of stress, ageing and worry
Slowing of the ageing process
Release of chronic headaches, shoulder pains etc
A more alive, healthy, relaxed appearance

A course of Rejuvanessence treatments comprises of six one-hour sessions, each working on different groups of connective tissue and muscles. As the treatment progresses and the therapist works on the deeper layers of the muscles, lines and wrinkles begin to diminish and the skin tone is firmed and improved.

Rejuvanessence is for both women and men. Even children benefit, showing positive changes in their faces, and greater calmness and harmony in their bodies.

The skin and ageing
The skin is made up of two layers, the epidermis, the outer layer which we can see and touch, and the dermis, usually called the connective tissue, the inner layer of fat that lies beneath the visible skin. Embedded in the connective tissue are the nerve endings, meridians, acupuncture points, collagen, lymph and blood vessels that carry oxygen to the cells in the epidermis, so that problems here will result in corresponding problems in the epidermis, as the cells become sluggish, so cutting down the flow of oxygen and blood to the skin cells. The

skin becomes lack-lustre in appearance, and, over time, the face becomes drawn and tight, ageing sets in, and lines begin to form.

The cells of the connective tissue secrete collagen fibres, that weave together to form a net-like structure. They also exude a gelatine-like substance that fills the space between the fibres. What we call ageing of the skin is in reality a stiffening and hardening of this substance, which can also cause the skin to 'glue' to the layers below it - to the connective tissue surrounding the muscles and bones of the face.

Rejuvanessence gently releases this 'glue', freeing the muscles and the connective tissue to restore skin tone and a more youthful appearance to the face. At the same time, the problems caused by long-held tension in the muscles (headache, jaw, neck .lr pain) are relieved, so that the energy flow in the body is balanced, the, tem fine-tuned and harmony of body and mind is restored.
For information about training, please contact Margareta Loughran on 020 7352 8458.

When Mary 45, decided on a course of treatments she felt pretty exhausted. Her face was showing the stress of time, lines and wrinkles began to set in. Skin looked tired and sallow. We had a brief look at her nutrition, facial care routine and water intake. During the treatments Mary would quickly fall into deeply relaxed state. As her body and facial muscles began to release tension and toxins her facial features began to change. She looked fresher and happier. More importantly the skin softened, lifted and plumped up. Wrinkles and lines appeared finer. Perfect alternative to surgery with out the trauma or expense, even my husband is impressed" she remarked. **By Bianca Mason**

Reyad Sekh Em

REYAD SEKH EM is an ultra high vibrational energy healing system. It uses a unique combination of the elemental healing rays of Earth, Water, Fire, Air and Spirit with ancient Egyptian symbolism and angelic philosophies.

We live in a multi-dimensional reality and many of us, consciously or unconsciously, shift in and out of various dimensions all the time. These other dimensions co-exist in the same physical space as ours. The separation between them is quite simply that each operates at a different vibratory level. Energy healing systems such as Reiki and Reyad Sekh Em allow access to these higher dimensions, giving the recipient a spiritual boost and helping nurture them towards greater wellbeing.

Reyad Sekh Em evolved from Tera Mai™ Reiki and Seichem. The spelling – Seichem, Sekh Em or SKHM – is purely arbitrary, because the Ancient Egyptians had no way of denoting vowels.

Sekh Em is listed in Middle Egyptian dictionaries as meaning 'make complete' or 'power'. Se Khem – another alternative spelling – would mean 'born of Khemit'. The Ancient Egyptians called their land Khemit, so this means 'born in Egypt', which is also very apt.

Reyad literally means 'elemental'. This addition to the name was suggested by Hakim, an Egyptian tribal elder who has been involved in the development of the system.

The Khemitians (Ancient Egyptians) believed that we all have the capacity to use 360 senses, rather than the five we now acknowledge. These other senses may be reawakened by self-empowerment activities, including positive intent, meditation, pilgrimages to key sacred sites and connecting with healing energies or the elements. All of these activities raise our vibratory rate and therefore can act as triggers for clairvoyance, clairsentience, clairaudience and many more additional 'senses'.

The system has evolved to include the use of self-empowerment meditations, etheric crystals, colour breathing and sound healing and also embraces angelic philosophies. A more recent addition is the shamanic-style negative energy drain technique, which facilitates the release of heavy, dense energy. The drain can help to tackle anything from emotional issues through arthritis and ME, to fertility problems and even cancers. Children with learning difficulties such as autism and ADHD have also responded favourably.

Reyad Sekh Em can be learned as a natural progression from Reiki or on its own. During initiation the sacred symbols of Kheper (the scarab, or dawn), Ra (the ram, or high noon), Oon (the wise, or early afternoon), Aten (the wiser, or late afternoon) and Amen (the hidden, veil or dusk) are placed into the aura at specific chakra points. For the ancient Egyptians the five-pointed star represented these five stages of the day, and of life itself, and also the elements of Earth, Water, Fire, Air and Ether, or Spirit.

The symbols cause a change in the energy field, enhancing the initiate's vibrational state and bringing them closer into touch with other dimensions and the loving guidance of beings within them. Once this has happened, it's up to the individual to decide how they will walk the path towards enlightenment.

Rolfing training begins with the ten session series that Dr. Rolf developed, and several variations of this protocol are taught. Over the years, the faculty of the Rolf Institute has articulated the principles on which the original series was based. By understanding these principles, it is possible for practitioners to develop strategies of intervention that recognize the unique needs of the individual client, and to work outside of the ten session series when appropriate.

Gentle Techniques - Because Rolfers work with the deep myofascial structures, some people can experience the work as uncomfortable. Rolfers have gradually developed a broad range of techniques that produce profound results with less discomfort for the client.

Joint Mobilization Techniques - The Rolf Institute faculty has created a range of soft tissue techniques to release articular motion restrictions that impede whole body organization. These skills increase the Rolfer's effectiveness in working with many common structural problems.

The Personal Experience - Because Rolfing is a holistic technique, it is recognized that changes in structure will impact the whole person, physically, emotionally, and energetically. The Rolf Institute recognizes that ultimately, it is the person's own experience of the work that is of primary importance. This plays a central role in the transformational aspect of Rolfing.

What is the difference between massage and Rolfing?

One of the most common misconceptions about Rolfing is that it is a nothing more than a type of very deep massage. There are many varieties of massage, which are particularly effective for loosening tight tissue, reducing stress, detoxing the body and an increased feeling of relaxation and well-being. Since these benefits are also a byproduct of Rolfing, the general public experience confusion as to the precise difference between our work and the proliferation of effective touch modalities currently available. Ray McCall, an Advanced Rolfer in Boulder and former student of Dr. Rolf, once said that what Rolfers do can be summed up in three words: palpation, discrimination and integration. We palpate, or touch the tissue, feeling for imbalances in tissue texture, quality and temperature to determine where we need to work. We discriminate, or separate fascial layers that adhere and muscles that have been pulled out of position by strain or injury. Finally, we integrate the body, relating its segments in an improved relationship, bringing physical balance in the gravitational field. Other soft-tissue manipulation methods, including massage, are quite good at the first two, but do not balance the body in gravity. As Dr. Rolf used to say: "Anyone can take a body apart, very few know how to put it back together." The true genius of her method is the art and science of reshaping and reorganizing human structure according to clearly defined principles in a systematic and consistent manner.

In addition to our skill as structural integrators, we are also educators, a point Dr. Rolf stressed frequently in her training classes. The role of teacher is something every Rolfer takes seriously. In each session, Rolfers seek to impart insights to clients to increase their awareness and understanding, to help the client make the work we do their own. Our job is to make ourselves obsolete, by empowering our clients to take charge of their own physical

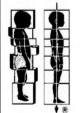

Rolfing

and emotional health. Influencing the structural evolution of man on a global level was Dr. Rolf's fondest dream.

My feet felt better than they had for about 25 years, and my body, while not quite 25 years younger, had stopped feeling old, caved in and stuck. I felt lighter, there was more space between my ribs and my internal organs, and things just seemed to be in the right place. My head and neck, which have long been sunk down and over arched, have become more supported and less clenched. At the end of the ten sessions, I feel as though I'm much closer to knowing what a normal, confident and supportive body feels like.
Female, mid-forties
Alan Richardson
www.alan-richardson.co.uk

'I was drawn to Rolfing by a desire to regain flexibility after a shoulder injury. Leisls initial assessment was attentive and reassuring and her enthusiasm infectious. The outcome has exceeded my wildest expectation- I have activated muscle groups neglected for years. The results are so tangible, after the sixth session I was suddenly able to swim a length in twelve strokes where previously in took fourteen. My core strength and posture have improved dramatically and the process of teaching my body how to move more ergonomically and gracefully seems to continue long after completing my ten sessions. I'd recommend her to anyone.' Amanda Perkins, Registered General Nurse.
By Leisl Hinkly, Certified Rolfer

Martin had suffered from chronic back pain for fifteen years and had tried everything to relieve the problem. After the first Rolfing session he found the pain was significantly reduced. By the sixth session the pain had gone, he felt lighter in his body and was moving with greater ease.
By Sue Over, Certified Rolfer

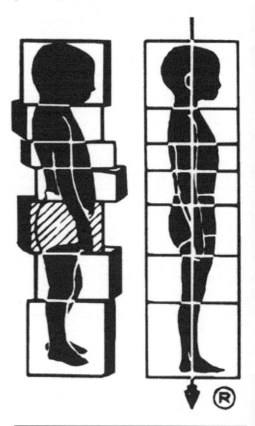

Shiatsu can be especially useful for postural problems, musculo-skeletal problems and any stress related illnesses, including emotional problems.

As might be expected from the link with and Chinese Medicine (either herbal or acupuncture), Shiatsu can be used to work with any or all of the disorders for which Acupuncture can be used. This is not to say that Shiatsu is the same as Acupuncture. Acupuncture may be thought of as being more specific and focussed than Shiatsu with regard to some ailments. However, as with many complementary therapies, some individuals (and some ailments) respond better to one therapy or another. So some persons will respond best to (or prefer) Shiatsu, while others benefit more from Acupuncture.

What is Shiatsu

Shiatsu is a form of bodywork that has its origins in Traditional Chinese Medicine and the historical massage techniques of Japan. Modern Shiatsu is based on these oriental traditions (which go back several thousand years) drawn tog ether with

ideas and knowledge from modern disciplines such as physiotherapy and psychology. These different disciplines were drawn together this century, mainly by the work of Shizotu Masunaga, to form what is now referred to as Zen Shiatsu. The focus of the Zen Shiatsu practitioner is to work with a client in the 'here and now', both giver and receiver having an 'active' involvement in what should become a meditative and intuitive process.

The term Shiatsu literally means "finger pressure" and as such only just begins to describe the work of the Shiatsu practitioner. In reality, various parts of the giver's body (fingers, thumbs, palms, forearms, even feet and knees) are used to apply pressure to the receiver's body. This can be targeted at general areas or specific points - often the tsubos or 'acu-points' used in acupuncture.

These techniques are used in conjunction with stretches, joint rotations and joint manipulation to give an 'all-over' treatment which aims at treating the receiver on a holistic level - working with body, mind and spirit together. Contacting the receiver's Ki or internal energy is an integral part of the treatment.Treatment is carried out fully clothed, usually with the receiver lying or sitting on a cushion on the ground.

Sound Therapy

Sound is defined as "The sensation resulting from stimulation of the auditory mechanism by air waves or vibrations".

Rattles, Musical Instruments, Human Voices, Drums Singing, Chanting, Crystal and Tibetan Bowls, Bells, Tin Shas, Tuning Forks and Frequency Generators are amongst the many instruments used in the field of sound Therapy. However they al have one thing in common; that is they produce sounds of varying natures.

The importance of sound to mankind has been shown by mans ingenuity to use the landscape as well as instruments to create or enhance sounds to promote physical and spiritual well being. This is evidenced by ancient Megalithic sites such as Newgrange in Ireland which have been proven to create complex resonances. These sites were used as places of healing as well as sites to commune with the spirits.

All matter vibrates and human beings are to fact. Each one of us has a unique overall resonance and in perfect health we resonate in harmony with our environment or planet as well as with the universe. When our body frequencies are in harmony the body is healthy and when out of harmony disease occurs.

There are a varied range of sound therapies from which to choose. For simplicity these have divided into two main areas.

Firstly the more natural and intuitive which uses instruments and sound producing objects including the human voice to tone or chant and produce a range of general sounds either individually or in combinations with simple instruments such as drums. This relatively simple approach to using sound replicates to some degree the ways of ancestors, and today these techniques are more involved in balancing the charkas or energy centres of the body. When combined with other therapies, effective and powerful healing can be created i.e energy healing with crystal bowls can clear the entire energy field of stress.

The second area of sound therapy is more scientific and uses technology to generate sound. Harmonic Health, Tomatis; Joudry; Samonas; and The Mozart Effect, are a few of the many techniques available in this category.

Each of these techniques has a unique quality which can set it aside from the others and would be more suited to certain conditions. For example Tomatis is an effective auditory stimulating therapy which involves re-educating the way we listen and then using active sound feedback readdresses the imbalances creating harmony once again. Tomatis has been effective in enhancing learning and has been used to treat autism. The Motzart Effect, Joudry, Samonas and the listening programme can be categorised together as they all may involve the use of specially filtered recordings.

Harmonic Health differs as it analyses the energy of the frequencies in the voice and can be very specific in determining what exact frequencies are incongruent, be they muscular or skeletal or biochemical and then by giving these frequencies back readdresses the balance in the body once more. This has bee very effective in pain management and muscular conditions.

By Jonathan D Cohen

"RG" is a 46 year old male. He had a chronic lower back, neck and pelvic pain for over 4 years which had not responded to treatment. Using the harmonic Health techniques of voice analysis, his voice patterns showed imbalances in L4 / L5, Gracilis, Psoas and gluteal muscles. Treatment using very low frenquency sound was carried out and he was pain free after one session and after further sessions he has made a full recovery.

Have you ever had a sense of knowledge from deep within your soul that we are not on our own and will never be? Have you ever felt a deep connection with everything around you and experienced unconditional love and compassion? Have you had times in your life where you felt that you didn't belong or didn't fit in? If this is you, then in these moments you have touched the divine or tapped into the spiritual potential deep within you. The truth is that we never walk alone, for we are here to learn and to follow our own very important journey which we call 'our life'. Sometimes it is rocky and sometimes it is amazing. Whatever the case our experiences are as valuable to us as the knowledge that we are being watched over and protected for most of our life by those in the spirit world who love us without exception and will continue to do so whatever we do. We cannot ever let them down, for they will love us forever. Imagine your life in this world if you know that death was not final and that life had a very important purpose.

Imagine if you were able to tap into the spirit world and ask for their help and their healing at any time. Wouldn't that just be awesome? If you have received your calling, then it may be time to develop your gift. To develop is to learn to look within for answers, and to do this you need to be focussed and in a state of deep relaxation. Meditation is the key! Learn to tune in and listen to your higher self and to the direction and guidance of your guides. There is a guide who most call their guardian, who will be with you throughout your lifetime, but there are other guides, companions and protectors who will come in and out of your life at periods of time when they are needed. You can learn to experience that wonderful feeling that you are never alone. You can develop a deeper spiritual understanding with the use of meditation, journeying, visualisation, prayer, positive thinking and sharing.

If you are a therapist, developing your intuition is essential, as you will be able to look at your clients and sense what is wrong with them. You must be able to help them emotionally as well as physically and they will feel an extra empathy with you which will encourage them to come back for further treatments. Through developing your intuition you can walk hand in hand with your spirit guides, guardian angels and those that love you from the spirit world. This is a path that goes

on and on, the excitement never goes away and your levels of consciousness rise continually, to the point where you can commune with an angel, you can tell your problems to your spirit guide, and you can ask for an easier or more settled life. Miracles happen to a great many people, it is just that half the time people are too busy to notice. Through spiritual enlightenment, you too can experience miracles as well as peace, tranquillity and unconditional love. Spiritual development is about creating a partnership of the right balance of energies to develop, helping your attunement to the world of spirit through inspiration, deepening your spirit presence, disciplined communication, protection, trust and help. By Debi Jay.

Spiritual Healing *is an expression of the love of God. Spiritual Healing is for the sick in mind, body or soul and/or any combination of all three. Thought, prayer and meditation can express Spiritual Healing. The patient can experience the benefit of healing whether in the presence of the Healer or not. Spiritual Healing is performed by the laying on of hands or by holding the hands*

close to the body of the patient without actually touching. *Spiritual Healing is not only for the relief of pain and disease; it is for the healing of the soul of the individual. Spiritual Healing passes through the healer to the patient and does not come directly from the healer.*

Text kindly donated by The Greater World Christian Spiritualist Association.

Palmistry
The study of the lines and signs of the hands.
Throughout our lifetime, our bodies register change. For example, the lines on our face that we acquire with age reflect experience and, we hope, wisdom. Lines and signs on our hands, present at birth, grow as we evolve, signifying the accumulated experience of our lives.

Centuries ago, the sages of India established a system of knowledge stemming from the Vedas, the earliest sacred Hindu writings. They studied the hands as a means to unveil and understand the self and relationships with others. They saw that the unique patterns of lines and signs in the hand come into being as a direct result of the way we think. Just as a pebble thrown into the water creates ripples, so our thoughts create similar effects.

Our hands offer us an objective view of who we really are. Through the study of palmistry, we have the opportunity to see to what extent our thoughts and feelings influence our happiness and the harmony of those around us. As we exercise our will in choosing positive patterns of thinking to replace any negative ones, we see our lines begin to change, reflecting a shift in our consciousness. As Shakespeare observed, we are masters of our own fate, that "the fault...is not in our stars, but in ourselves."

Traditional Thai Yoga Massage or Nuad Thai evolved in Thailand around 2000 years ago alongside Buddism with its roots lying in ayurvedic medicine and yoga philosophy. The massage is a flowing, structured combination of acupressure and applied yoga stretches. The whole body is treated from the top of the head to the tips of the fingers and toes leaving both the mind and body feeling balanced, free and flexible. By instilling equilibrium and harmony better health can be achieved.

Although the massage often appeals to those who practise yoga, it can benefit anyone, whatever their level of fitness, state of health or age. The massage is tailor-made to meet each persons needs and abilities.

The massage focuses on ten energy lines, or Sen lines, through which the lifeforce, prana, circulates around pathways in the body. It is believed that blockages within the flow will result in pain, illness or disease. The lines are thoroughly worked with slow rhythmic compressions and with stretching. This ensure that prana flows freely and any blocked energy is released restoring balance, harmony and, consequently health and well-being. By the end of the massage the receiver feels physically more flexible and relieved of tension as well as balanced, energised and revived.

The therapist may use her hands, thumbs, elbows and feet to apply the pressure and then her whole body in order to create the yoga stretches. The massage is never rushed taking an hour and a half to two hours and is given in a rhythmic, flowing manner which encourages the release of tension. It is has even been described as dance-like. In true Thai tradition, the massage is applied as a meditative practice and given with metta or loving kindness.

The treatment is ideal for the relief of stresses and muscular tension but it also improves flexibility and strength. By rebalancing the body's energetic system, natural healing processes are encouraged and internal organs can function better, pain can be relieved and circulation improved. People often notice an increased awareness of posture, deeper more relaxed breathing and a feeling of lightness and looseness.

Thai massage has been proven to be very effective in treating back pain, sciatica, neck and shoulder pain, knee pain, headaches, asthma, general fatigue, menstrual difficulties and many other ailments. It has been found to be particularly helpful to those who are paralysed or have MS. In fact, in Thailand thai yoga massage is often recommended in preference to conventional medicine for recovery after a stroke.

The massage is especially beneficial during pregnancy and after giving birth. A complete massage can be given with the receiver lying on their side during later stages of pregnancy or for anyone who has a problem lying on their back.

There are no particular requirements of the receipient only that loose comfortable clothing is worn so that movement is unrestricted since the massage is carried out on a futon-type mat on the floor. Occasionally oil or balm is used on painful areas.

Carol Garrison
Tel: 020 8530 8975 or 07939 484 017

Therapeutic Healing

Therapeutic touch is a method in which the hands are used to "direct human energies to help or heal someone who is ill." Proponents claim that the patient's "energy field" can be detected and intentionally manipulated by the therapist. They theorize that healing results from a transfer of "excess energy" from healer to patient. Their reports claim that TT is effective against scores of diseases and conditions.

Therapeutic Touch was conceived in the early 1970s by Dolores Krieger, Ph.D., R.N., a faculty member at New York University's Division of Nursing. The "human energy field" TT theorists postulate resembles the "magnetic fluid" or "magnetic force" hypothesized during the 18th century by Anton Mesmer and his followers [1]. Mesmerism held that illnesses are caused by obstacles to the free flow of this fluid and that skilled healers ("sensitives") could remove these obstacles by making passes with their hands. Some aspects of mesmerism were revived in the nineteenth century by Theosophy, an occult religion that incorporated Eastern metaphysical concepts and underlies many current "New Age" ideas. Dora Kunz, who is considered TT's co-developer, was president of the Theosophical Society of America from 1975 to 1987. She collaborated with Krieger on the early TT studies and claims to be a fifth-generation "sensitive" and a "gifted healer."

Today's proponents state that more than 100,000 people worldwide have been trained in TT technique, including at least 43,000 health care professionals, and that about half of those trained actually practice it. TT generally involves four steps: (1) "centering," a meditative process said to align the healer with the patent's energy level, (2) "assessment," said to be performed by using one's hands to detect forces emanating from the patient, (3) "unruffling the field," said to involve sweeping "stagnant energy" downward to prepare for energy transfer, and (4) transfer of "energy" from practitioner to patient. "Non-contact therapeutic touch" is done the same way, except that the "healer's" hands are held a few inches away from the body. TT is sometimes used together with massage.

There is no scientific evidence that the "energy transfer" postulated by proponents actually occurs. It is safe to assume that any reactions to the procedure are psychological responses to the "laying on of hands."

Sarah had chronic fatigue and ill health for several years. Flare-ups would occur during times of stress. After receiving regular sessions of therapeutic healing she learnt to listen to her body more and found she could manage her energy better on a daily basis. The sessions also helped her to begin to deal with old emotional issues which were part of the bigger picture in her health's deterioration.
By Linda Hall

Despite the grand name of THERMO-AURICULAR© THERAPY, the therapy is the use of 'candles' which are in fact hollow tubes made in the traditional Hopi Indian way by using a combination of herbal extracts such as Sage (Salvia Officinalis), Chamomile (Matricaria Chamomile) and St. John's Wort (Hypericum Perforatum), which are blended in honey, organically grown linen and beeswax

Consulting a qualified Thermo-Auricular© therapist may not be the first thing that you think of to treat ear, nose and throat problems, but maybe you should, conditions including migraine and headaches, glue ear in children, catarrh, sore throats, colds, sinusitis, tonsillitis, 'flu and excessive ear wax have all been helped by their use.

During the treatment the candles work in three phases, the first being a chimney effect where a gentle suction, draws out debris from the ear. Next, the mild heat stimulates the blood and lymph circulation, boosting the immune system, therefore boosting the body's natural cleansing action. Finally a regulation of the pressure within the sinuses.

If you have either never heard of this therapy, or, would like to try the treatment however you are worried about being burnt, if you consult a qualified therapist (T.A.Th) you will be in safe hands. The candles have a filtering system and no residue can enter the ear. You will feel a warming sensation but the overall effect is very gentle and extremely relaxing.
Many people report an immediate release of pressure in their head after just one treatment session although; depending on the condition, three sessions may be required to ease an ongoing problem fully.
A session of THERMO-AURICULAR© THERAPY will begin with the therapist asking questions relating to you and your medical history, checking the ears for any infections or visible problems, performing the therapy and concludes with a massage of the face and ear area, totaling about 45 minutes.

Article donated by: Lynda Stokes and Sue Maunsell who are qualified in the use of Ear candles since 1989 and has received tuition from Birgit Ernst from BIOSUN the manufacturers in Germany.

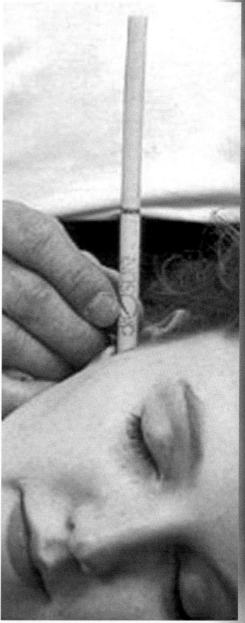

Transendental Meditation

Imagine- if just sitting quietly in a comfortable chair for a few minutes of very enjoyable deep relaxation every day could leave you feeling mentally and physically refreshed, with a calmer and more alert mind, increased energy and clearer thinking.

As a result you found that you could achieve more with less effort, that your deepest desires began to find fulfillment and that work, recreation and relationships were more rewarding.

These are some of the benefits gained by more than six million people who are practising Transcendental Meditation ("TM").

Teacher Cohn Beckley explains: "Many people say that they 'find it hard to make their minds be still', often having tried (or even taught) many different forms of meditation. They are surprised and delighted to find after learning TM that with the right technique and a proper understanding it is very easy, not to make the mind still, but to allow it to settle down towards peace.

During TM the mind settles to its most silent and restful state and yet remains fully alert. In this peaceful, often blissful state of self awareness, the body also gains very deep rest, much deeper than in sleep, (called by scientists a 'restructuring state') which allows the body's natural healing mechanisms to function fully.

Deep-rooted stresses and tensions are spontaneously dissolved, bringing relief to a wide range of health problems. Mental health is improved as the conditioning caused by past experience is dissolved and we spontaneously begin to live with joy and freedom in the present moment.

"If TM were a new drug, it would be hailed as a major break-through" Dr N Argyle, Consultant psychiatrist

Sensory experience is enhanced. Artists report increased appreciation of colour and musicians an extra delight in sound. Many others report taste and smells coming to life. Increased enjoyment of sex is common and fertility has been known to improve.

People of all professions rediscover their natural ability to remain calm under pressure, free from tension and fatigue and at the peak of their mental clarity and performance, which has encouraged companies such as Sony, General Motors, IBM, and Toyota to make TM available to their staff.

"The overall benefits of regular TM are so staggering as to be almost unbelievable- in one 5 year study, half the number of in-patient admissions to hospital (87% fewer for heart disease and nervous system disorders). These findings are remarkable"
Dr James Le Fanu in the Sunday Telegraph

You might expect something with such wide ranging benefits would be difficult to do, but TM is easy: so effortless it can be practised on a train or bus or in a busy airport.

By Colin Beckley Independent Teacher of Transcendental Meditation, The College of Meditation. www.tm-meditation.co.uk

Yoga

Yoga originated in India as a philosophy and practice for Self-awareness, leading to health and harmony of mind, body and spirit. Even in the 21st century Yoga techniques produce the same benefits – improving the functioning of the body and developing a more calm and balanced outlook on life.

If you have never tried Yoga before, or want to change your practice, it is important to find the right teacher for your needs. There are many different types of Yoga, so what do you want?
● A challenging physical practice?
● Gentle exercise and relaxation to suit age, ability, lifestyle?
● Spiritual development?
● Therapy and education to manage a variety of physical conditions, injuries, trauma, mental or emotional distress?
● A combination of these?
● Group classes or individual tuition?
● A class on a particular day and time? (This might be the deciding factor!!)

As an exercise system for gaining and maintaining flexibility and fitness, Yoga offers active and passive stretching in a variety of postures and sequences ranging from simple to challenging. Shape, weight, age and ability are not restrictive once you have chosen the right class for your needs. A good teacher will guide you with appropriate modifications to suit your capabilities and requirements.

Busy lives mean that we need to find time to relax both in body and mind. It can be difficult to switch off. The physical practices of Yoga can help the body to relax and meditation helps the mind. Becoming aware of how we breathe is very important for both. Yoga breathing techniques can lead to improvements in posture, health and concentration. Regular practice can minimise the effects of stress and ill-health. The body's immune system begins to work better and as a consequence we feel happier, healthier and have an improved quality of life.

Yoga can also help when people feel "disabled" or restricted in everyday activities. The causes might be chronic or systemic illnesses, accidents and operations which often limit movement and confidence. As well as physical problems there might also be emotional stress and pain caused by terminal illness, addictions, low self-esteem, learning difficulties, bereavement or trauma, in such cases more specific, personalised practices can help people focus on their abilities and potential in order to manage such disturbances and improve the quality of life.

For over 40 years the British Wheel of Yoga has promoted the teaching and enjoyment of yoga. Other yoga organisations provide similar support. To find out more about yoga or teachers in your area contact the Central Office of the British Wheel of Yoga on 01529 306851 or visit www.bwy.org.uk.

Simon Owen- Teacher of Yoga and Alexander Technique, Tel: 07973 523237 www.yoga-breaks.com See main advertisement under Alexander Technique on page 5.

Clinics & Centres

Decisions about your health care are important-including decisions about whether to use complementary and alternative medicine (CAM).

Take charge of your health by being an informed consumer. Find out what scientific studies have been done on the safety and effectiveness of the CAM treatment in which you are interested.

Decisions about medical care and treatment should be made in consultation with a health care provider and based on the condition and needs of each person. Discuss information on Complementary & Alternative Medicine (CAM) with your health care provider before making any decisions about treatment or care.

If you use any CAM therapy, inform your primary health care provider. This is for your safety and so your health care provider can develop a comprehensive treatment plan.

If you use a CAM therapy provided by a practitioner, such as acupuncture, choose the practitioner with care. Check with your insurer to see if the services will be covered.

Alexandria Healing Centre, 39 Alexandria Road, London, W13 0NR, London, 0208 579 7230
info@alexandriahealing.co.uk
www.alexandriahealing.co.uk
see main advert under Kinesiology on page 39.

School of Light, 12 Woodberry Grove, London, N12 0DL, 0208 4466627   see main advert under Sound Therapy on page 64.

Previous participants have said:
"If only biology had been taught like this at school!" "[Your course] took my understanding of the human body further than I would have thought possible in just two weekends. I was filled with wonder at the complexity and beauty ...."
"Amazing — fabulous way of learning!"
"I feel a greater sense of my body through the gentle process." "You have given me keys to my inner world." "Motivating and inspiring teacher."
Testimonials provided by Body Knowledge Body Wisdom

Beginning Spring 2006
Diploma in Living Harmony
Two year part-time course for:
Professional Training and Personal Enhancement

While respecting the uniqueness, yet interconnectedness of all, this course teaches you to embrace the latest findings of Energy Medicine and Science, and re-awakens your innate abilities to sense and correct energy disturbances in yourself, others and the environment
● Accredited by the AET and affiliated to the BCMA ●

For more details, please contact Val Bullen:
valbullen@aol.com, tel: 01749 870 026
or Viviane Fingerhut: vfingerhut@onetel.com,
tel: 020 8958 17 40

Body Journeys

Come on guided explorations of your body to learn about its structure and function, and to experience its healing wisdom

Accredited professional Anatomy and Physiology training courses

Personal and professional development workshops and groups

Individual '*Integrative Healing*' sessions

For 2005-06 programme contact:

Jen Altman
MA, PhD, ITEC, Dip Ther. Healing

01706 839878
Jennifer.altman@boltblue.com
or see: www.ath.org.uk

HEALING ANGELS

Offers a variety of certificated courses & workshops to promote Spiritual Growth, Personal Development & Self Healing.

Would you like to spend a short break (including weekends) connecting with your Angels & guides? Healing with the Angels? increasing your Spiritual Awareness and Psychic potential. Developing your Self Healing skills? Or unlocking the door to healing your past life and much much more?

If so please contact Lindy on 01626 865897 or 07837217283 Email linda.spencer2@tesco.net

MyoTherapeia Courses

FACT: **90% of clients would prefer a deeper and more skilful massage than what they currently receive**

FACT: **MyoTherapeia gives you the skills you need to offer a proper deep tissue massage and advice on back care that clients need**

MyoTherapeia is an innovative deep tissue massage technique based on 12 anatomy and physiology principles.

Understanding those principles will give you the confidence and expertise you need to create your own winning remedial massage formula based on your clients needs.

Private and small group classes and workshops are available in Kensington, London or on-site at your spa/salon.

For more information you may contact:
08450 573112
or visit: www.myotherapeia.com

Products & Services

Health maintenance and cancer treatment support

Rated the top TCM herb for 2000 years, Reishi is now the most thoroughly researched with over 200 active and unique compounds proven to provide an extraordinary range of health supporting benefits. Reishi is called 'The Long Life Herb' and 'The Great Protector' for good reasons.

Treasured in Asia as a 'life extender' superior to Ginseng, Cordyceps is now available in the West. The Health Science Institute stated Cordyceps is an 'Extraordinary remedy, dramatically boosting energy levels, improving cardiac and respiratory health, relieving ailing kidneys and supporting the immune system'.

A major cancer research organisation affirm that these compounds have a remarkable ability to reduce the debilitating effects of traditional cancer treatments.

Personally sourced in China, Lifeforce concentrated extracts contain the highest levels of active ingredients in the world.

www.liferce-herbs.co.uk 0845 060 0052.

Products & Services

Essences of Life

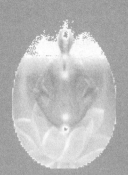

Catherine Pritchard Healing Practitioner has developed a unique way of channelling Personal Essences and Remedies for each individual. By tuning into the energy field of each person or animal and finding which healing energies are needed. This technique is especially helpful as each essence and remedy is tailored for each personal case, Emotionally, Mentally, Physically, and Spiritually.

Catherine has many years of experience as a healing practitioner, she is skilled in balancing and harmonising the emotional, mental, physical and spiritual bodies, facilitating the removal of trauma that blocks the individual from their true life path.

For more information contact:
Catherine Pritchard,
Essences of Life
Cranberry Bungalow, Poolspringe,
Llanwarne, Much Birch,
Hereford HR2 8JJ
01981 541124/ 07817 416984
Email. Cath@essencesoflife.co.uk

Directory

Directory

Directory

NATURAL WELLNESS.

Sedentary life style choices, obesity, stress, convenience foods, over indulgent consumerism are indicative of the characteristics of the 21st.Century, so at a time when the health of the nation is becoming an ethical and political issue, the need to find ways of living a healthier and more prolonged life has acquired a special urgency. That quest is the purpose of this book.

This book connects those who want complementary & alternate medicine with those who can provide it: therapists, product and service providers, schools and colleges, and a whole range of professionals concerned with complementary medicine. With in excess of 100 therapy explanations by experts and a directory of professional therapists it offers an authoritative guide to many of the therapies available. It will become an invaluable tool in the search for treatment and cure using natural sciences.

Priced at only £7.95
It is a book that many of us have longed for.

To speed find a therapist in your area visit –
www.naturalhealthdirect.com

The Natural Wellness can be ordered from a W.H. Smith shop, any quality High Street book shop or direct from **ABA Distribution. 59 College Road. Keyham. Plymouth PL2 1NT. When ordering please quote ISBN 0-9526555-8-6.**

Holistic Insights titles currently available:

South West includes Bristol – Somerset – Wiltshire – Dorset – Devon & Cornwall.

South & South East includes Hampshire – Sussex E & W – Surrey & Kent.

Thames & Chilterns includes Bedfordshire – Buckinghamshire – Hertfordshire – Oxfordshire & Berkshire – Somerset – Wiltshire – Dorset – Devon & Cornwall.

The Midshires includes Nottinghamshire – Leicestershire – Derbyshire – Staffordshire – Northamptonshire & West Midlands..

London Regions includes Central & Greater London.

Next edition due Spring 2006 - *West Midlands & Northwest Counties.*

Due Autumn 2006 - *Yorkshire & Northeast Counties.*

Due Winter 2006 - *East Anglia.*

Other Complementary & Alternative health books available from
ABA Distribution: Telephone 01752 519747.

The Green Life (Foreword by Richard Briers OBE) a mixture of natural health therapies and environmental subjects. Price £7.95 + £4.00 p & p.

Natural Health Directory (Foreword by Jenny Agutter) over 400 pages of therapies & therapists situated throughout the UK. Price £7.95 + £4.00 p&p.

All credit cards taken except AMEX & Diners.

To speed find a therapist in your area please visit: www.naturalhealthdirect.com